Baby & Family

cook for family, adapt for baby

Baby & Family

cook for family, adapt for baby

BY SIOBHAN BERRY

MummyCooks.com

© Mummy Cooks by Siobhan Berry, 2018
978-1-78808-058-3

Photography by Dave Berry & Shika Finnemore
Designed by Shika Finnemore
Illustrations by Shika Finnemore
Printed in Italy by L.E.G.O. SpA

A CIP Catalogue record of this book is available from the British library.

www.MummyCooks.com

All content in this book is not intended to be a substitute for professional medical advice. Always seek the advice of your paediatrician or other qualified health provider with any concerns you may have about introducing foods to your baby.

**To my beautiful girls,
Ashleigh and Jessica**

**My little foodies, I am so proud
of you both.**

My charity partner

———— ••• ————

I am delighted to have partnered with the NMH Foundation to raise much needed funds to support the work of the National Maternity Hospital, Holles Street, with special attention given to the Neonatal Care Unit. I will donate 10% of the book profits to the NMH foundation.

My birth experience...

I was fortunate to have had two positive birth experiences. This was due to a little bit of luck and the great support and care from all the staff at Holles Street Hospital. Thankfully the birth of my first daughter Ashleigh went well, so I was able to avail of the wonderful Community Midwifery Service by Holles Street Hospital for my second pregnancy. Again, the care I received was fabulous right from the start. I met with midwives all the way through my pregnancy, and my second daughter Jessica was born in the Hospital by the assistance of a Domino midwife. As soon as she was checked, we were on our way home. The midwives then visited me regularly over the next few days and they were a great support, especially helping me to establish breastfeeding. It was such a positive experience and one of the great services that the NMH has to offer. I am delighted to be in a position to give back because as the saying goes, 'a good start is half the work'.

Dr Rhona Mahony, Master of National Maternity Hospital Holles St.

Being a parent is a journey for which few of us can be fully prepared for. As doctors, midwives and other health professionals working in our maternity hospitals, we work hard to provide the care and guidance to prepare parents as best we can for birth and bringing baby home. Being a new parent can be a daunting experience with so much to learn from feeding to sleeping, to finding ways to help our little ones grow and develop to achieve their full potential. Introducing your baby to solid foods is a new adventure, and one with plenty of thrills and spills. Siobhan's guide to weaning and her tasty recipes, will help every new parent embark on this stage of development with ease and confidence. I am so happy that this book will not only aid parents to feed their children healthy, nutritious first foods, but the National Maternity Hospital Foundation will benefit too with a 10% charity contribution from every book sold.

Acknowledgements

I want to say a huge thank you to all the Mummy Cooks Mums who have attended my classes or cooked my recipes. The positive feedback I have received has spurred me on to write this book. When mums tell me that I have in some way had a positive impact on feeding their child it gives me the drive to keep spreading the word and help new mums starting out. The Mummy Cooks journey has been a pleasure, thank you all for making it possible.

To my husband, you have encouraged and supported me throughout this journey. Your creative input and stunning photography has given our girls the most amazing memories of their childhood through your camera lens and your sense of adventure. Thank you to my two girls, my tasters. I love you both so much.

To my own Mum, you always told me that I could be anything I want to be. Thank you for instilling in me a love of cooking and thank you for always having a warm nourishing meal on the table. I will always have memories of when I went travelling and all I wanted was your dinner.

To the Mummy Cooks team, over the last four years who have come and gone, thank you for your help and support. A special thanks to the very talented Shika, who has made this recipe book into a reality. Your amazing food photography and illustrations have made it into something to be very proud of. I wish you every success.

To my sister Catriona, Paediatric Occupational Therapist. You are a big part of why I set up Mummy Cooks. I thank you so much for all your help and advice when I was coming up with the concept and your expert advice on how to help mums feed their babies. Love you to bits.

And to my friend Tara Hayes, I really appreciate the effort you went to in editing this book. Thank you so much for making it ready for print. You have a new calling!

Testimonials from our Mummy Cooks Mums

―――――― ••• ――――――

"Our MummyPages mums always crave advice and inspiration when it comes to feeding their family and weaning is no different. We find that our first time mums in particular, lack confidence when it comes to navigating the different stages and challenges that present themselves as their baby grows and develops. Through her role teaching weaning classes to mums of young babies and as an expert for our website, Siobhan has empowered thousands of mums to create their own meals from scratch and nurture their children's growing interest in and appetite for food.

With so much conflicting advice from generations of parents and well-meaning friends, it is wonderful to finally have a trusted resource to refer our mums to when it comes to embarking on their weaning journey. In this must-read book, Siobhan has distilled the current advice honed by doctors, occupational therapists, dietitians, nutritionists, and the World Health Organisation into an easy step-by-step guide for parents who want to raise children with a positive attitude to all foods. The delicious recipes will not only be devoured by parents looking to create a well-balanced diet for their little ones, but by the whole family too. With tips on preparation, portion sizes, batch cooking and freezing, this cookbook will be every mum's best friend when it comes to feeding their family from infant to family meals."

- Laura Erskine
Mum-in-Residence, MummyPages.ie

"I attended the baby weaning class with my 5½ month old son. We really enjoyed the morning, which was relaxed and educational all in one! As well as great food ideas, Siobhan also gave us mums lots of practical common sense advice about portion sizes, the rules of freezing food, hygiene and how to continually progress your baby's exposure to lots of different foods and textures. Siobhan demonstrated both finger and puréed foods, which we all sampled and took home in our pots for our babies to try later too. Following the class I felt much more confident to introduce a wider range of food types. My take home message was that baby can have (and should have!) the food we are eating at home made to the appropriate consistency in line with their stage of development. I really appreciated Siobhan's follow up email with further advice and great recipes too! Since the class my son has enjoyed every vegetable and fruit combination imaginable and is about to embark on protein and gluten - we can't wait!"

- Sinead O'Donnell
Paediatric Doctor and Mum to Killian

"MummyCooks.com is my go-to website when I need some inspirations for feeding the children. The ideas for lunches and quick family meals are just brilliant. All the meals are carefully designed to be healthy and balanced - it's such a relief not to have to think about it just follow the instructions!! It amazes me what children will actually eat that I wouldn't have thought to try without Mummy Cooks' advice.

I've been using the portion pots for ages now - they are such handy sizes not just for the weaning stages but for all family leftovers and freezer meals. I love that they are BPA free and also that all the sizes stack together so take up hardly any space in my packed cupboards!"

- Abigale Moore
Paediatric Dentist and Mum to Felicity

"I just wanted to say thanks for a wonderful weaning class. Not only are your products fantastic your classes are too and I will be recommending them to my friends and patients when I return back to work. I really learned a lot.... I feel I have gained a lot of confidence from your class. So thank you so much. Keep up the good work!

- Laura Reynolds
Pharmacist and Mum to Aideen

"I love the online recipes and portion guides. I find Mummy Cooks to be the best resource for weaning. I would highly recommend."

- Natasha Milan
Accountant and Mum to Patrick

"Thank you Siobhan for all your help and advice...it was truly invaluable! I was a little lost in the world of weaning but with Mummy Cooks help and delicious recipes, I'm feeling so much more confident about it all..."

- Sharlene Leonard
Optician and Mum to Odhrán

"I get a lot of inspiration from MummyCooks.com. We have tried the Coconut Chicken Curry and the Butternut Squash Risotto almost two years ago when I was weaning my second child and now four babies later and those two recipes are staples in our home. Plates demolished every single time, even daddies."

- Kellie Kearney
Blogger at My Little Babog, and Mum of four

"Left over chicken stew ready for freezer – if you're cooking for baby Mummy Cooks portion pots are the best!"

- Pippa O'Connor Ormond
Blogger, Entrepreneur and Mum to Ollie & Louis

Contents

Mummy Cooks by Siobhan Berry

My weaning experience...

Having your first child is an exciting, yet daunting, time as everything is so new. When I had my first daughter, Ashleigh, I was really passionate about giving her the best. This led to me pushing myself too hard and following ridiculous meal plans that required hours in the kitchen to prepare her food.

I soon learned that feeding a baby is much like feeding a family and I decided to start including her in our family meals. With the whole family eating the same meals, I could batch cook our dinners, snacks and her finger foods in advance. When my second child Jessica came along, weaning was a breeze!

After talking to other mothers, I found many were struggling to feed their children. This lead to me wondering why my girls happily accepted a range of new foods with no fuss, whilst other children were becoming picky eaters. At first, I thought this was associated with using shop bought food but this wasn't always the case. Mums spending hours in the kitchen still had a fussy eater.

I started to do some research and enlisted the help of my sister, a Paediatric Occupational Therapist. Our findings proved the importance of the weaning stages in raising an adventurous and healthy eater.

My food philosophy...

I began teaching weaning classes aimed at guiding parents on how to feed their babies. My message has always been that weaning is as much about the psychology of food as it is about the food that you offer to your baby. I am a big believer that taking a calm and relaxed approach will provide your baby with a better feeding experience.

"weaning before one is just for fun"

In this book, I provide parents with the tools to raise a healthy eater and to combat fussy eating stages. I cannot guarantee that your child will eat all the food if you follow my guide. My children are great eaters but it still takes a few attempts to convince them to try out new things. The first time it's almost always a no. The next time, it's usually not as scary, and soon, they are eating it like every other meal they enjoy.

My advice is drawn from my experience as a Mum feeding my two girls, and from my weaning classes where I meet a wide variety of parents and children, some just starting out and others who have a fussy child. The solutions I provide almost always work. Frequently, at the end of my weaning classes, I am asked where my book is. Well, here it is!

The Food Adventure Begins

————— ••• —————

I look on with envy when first-time mums come to my class about to embark on feeding their baby solid food for the first time. My own experience was such an exciting adventure. I always encourage mums at my class to think about feeding their baby as a journey and think less about what or how much they are eating. Breast or formula milk can provide up to half a baby's energy intake by the age of one. It is important to encourage your child to eat, but it's just as important to stay patient and not panic if they skip, or only eat half, of their meal.

Approach to weaning - Traditional vs. Baby led weaning...

There are two main schools of thought when it comes to feeding your child. The first, *traditional weaning* includes a combination of purées and finger food. The second, *baby-led weaning,* is where you let your baby feed themselves from the beginning. Both techniques can have similar outcomes, as long as your baby is given control while eating. Offering finger foods, in both methods, for your baby to pick up and eat gives them the experience of touching, feeling and bringing the food to their own mouth. Usually, it results in children feeling happy and enjoying the experience of mealtimes.

Traditional weaning can become a negative experience when parents don't give any control to their baby and insist on spoon feeding them purées. The problem with this approach is that the baby never sees the colour or feels the texture of the food. Some parents also employ a distraction as a tool to encourage eating something which I do not recommend! I advise giving a small portion of food to your baby so that they can touch, feel and attempt to bring it to their own mouth.

Please see *page 10* for a more information on how to give baby control.

Variety & Texture...

The key to a successful weaning journey is to offer a variety of tastes and textures from an early age.

Traditional weaning is based on a gradual increase in texture, starting with purées building up to minced and mashed foods. It also incorporates finger foods as a main meal or part of a meal *(pg 20)*. I always suggest that if your baby is hungry after their portion of food then it's best not to give them more of the same meal. Instead offer a finger food like apple slices. This mixes things up within the same mealtime.

Playing with different combinations of ingredients is another great way to add variety. When starting off, you can do this by batch cooking and storing individual vegetables or fruit purées separately. Then, all you have to do is mix different combinations together at mealtimes. When moving onto family meals, batch cook recipes, such as my Mediterranean Baked Cod *(pg 109)*. Each time you serve it, alternate a different carbohydrate accompaniment, such as pasta, potato, couscous or quinoa.

For more information about including variety and texture, see page 14.

Baby-Led Weaning...

Baby-led weaning (BLW) is becoming more popular. It really is the new buzz word when it comes to weaning. The cornerstone of this method is that you only offer finger foods to your baby, instead of spoon-fed purées. Unlike traditional weaning, you can only start BLW at six months of age, when your baby has lost their tongue-thrust reflex. If you feel that BLW is for you then follow your gut and go for it. If you are in anyway anxious then I would advice you stick to a combination of purées and finger food.

All of our recipes in this book have been carefully selected so they can be prepared as a finger food or as a purée. See more on how to introduce meals as finger foods on *page 20*.

Starting to Wean

The transition to solid foods can be tricky. It can also be messy, but it can definitely be a lot of fun. There are a lot of misconceptions about acceptable foods and how and when to start. I hope to ease you through this and set you up for a positive and happy weaning journey.

When to start weaning...

I recommend starting to wean between 5 and 5½ months. This allows you a few weeks to introduce some simple purées and to get your baby used to a lot of different tastes before you really engage with the process at 6 months.

This ensures that by 6 months your baby is ready for:

- Three meals a day
- New textures e.g. meat, fish & grains *(pg 17)*
- Finger foods *(pg 20)*
- Gluten foods *(pg 16)*

When exactly you decide to start will depend on your baby's individual development. However, there are guidelines you need to follow:

- Don't start before 4 months (17 weeks).
- If you start before 6 months, do not reduce the volume of breast or formula milk.
- Don't delay past 7 months as babies are more accepting of new foods at 6 months.
- The later you get started, the more likely they are to reject foods and become a fussy eater.

Signs your baby is ready...

1 They sit up well without support. High chairs are designed for older babies so use cushions to keep your baby in the right position. I always recommend starting to feed a younger baby on your lap, to ensure support.

2 They start to demand feeds more often and it seems like milk alone is not enough to sustain them.

3 They start to wake up during the night to feed having previously slept through the night.

4 They have lost their tongue-thrust reflex and no longer push solids out of their mouth. You will only know this once you try feeding your baby. If they thrust all the food out then they are not physically ready.

5 They start to eye up your food at mealtimes and seem keen to try food. This is a good sign your baby is ready, so don't be afraid to read their cues.

Weaning Checklist

Everything you will need to see you through your baby's entire weaning journey.

Storage Pots

Storage pots are essential when weaning your baby. It's not practical to cook every day. Having food in the freezer makes it easier for you to offer a variety of homemade meals throughout the week. My Mummy Cooks weaning pots are designed to help you portion correctly during each of your baby's development stages. You get enough pots to batch cook and they are translucent so you can easily see what food you've stored inside!

30ml/1oz
4-6m

60ml/2oz
6-7m

90ml/3oz
7-8m

120ml/4oz
8-9m

180ml/6oz
9-12m

Spoons

At 4 months, start off with soft shallow plastic spoons with long handles to feed your baby. From 6 months, use a shorter spoon so baby can hold it themselves to self-feed. This will enable them to develop utensil skills from an early age. Use spoons with soft tips to protect sensitive gums.

Bowls

Place a bowl with some food in front of your baby from 6 months of age. This will give them the control to self-feed, making their experience more enjoyable. Babies love to play

with their food as well as pick up their bowls, so a durable bowl is essential. To keep things a little less messy, use a suction bowl that will stick to baby's table. This will stop it from being thrown around like a frisbee!

Steamer

The best way to prepare vegetables for your baby is to steam them as this locks in key nutrients which can be lost when boiled.

Blender

Depending on your baby's weaning stage, you need to blend their food down to the required consistecy. To do this, you can use a blender, food processor or baby food grinder.

Beaker

Encourage your baby to drink from a beaker from 6 months. Fill it up with fresh filtered tap water and place it on the table with all meals. Choose a beaker with a soft, pliable spout to start off. If your baby refuses one type of cup, keep trying until you have found the perfect one. Your baby will get enough liquid from breast or bottle. The introduction of a beaker is to ensure they accept it as part of their feeding routine and enable them to move onto a beaker or cup from 12 months.

Highchair

Keep your baby in an upright position when feeding them, so they are able to swallow food properly. It's essential to get a secure, comfortable and washable high chair to feed your baby.

Food Flasks

My Mummy Cooks Food Flask is perfect for carrying food when you are out and about with your baby. For smaller babies I would advise placing your weaning pots inside to keep food warm or cold for up to 6 hours.

Cleaning & Care of my Mummy Cooks weaning pots

DISHWASHER   STERILISER   MICROWAVE

PVC FREE   BPA FREE   FREEZER

Wash in warm soapy water and then air dry before using for the first time and after each use.

My pots are top shelf dishwasher safe. If they fill up with water, simply empty out then rinse and air dry. They can also be used in a steamer to defrost food.

Getting Started

—— ... ——

Your baby's first foods should be smooth and easy to digest; think very runny purées of a single fruit or vegetable. This allows your baby to get used to solid food without being overwhelmed. It also allows you to introduce new textures and flavours one at a time for the first week or so. Remember, babies can vary in terms of how long it takes to accept solids. Some will accept them straight away, while others may take several weeks.

You don't need to follow a 3-day rule to introduce new foods. Only avoid foods if you or your partner has an allergy to them.

First tastes...

Your baby's very first foods must be easy to digest, so start with a runny and smooth texture, with no lumps. You can achieve this by cooking your fruit or vegetables for a little longer than your own. Add a little of the reserved water or baby's milk when blending to make it even smoother.

Foods to start...

Start by offering purées of root vegetables such as carrot, parsnip and sweet potato. If your baby doesn't accept the food off a spoon, try placing the food on your (clean) finger and let them suck it off. Once they are used to the taste and texture of the food, you can then reintroduce the spoon.

Check out my First Foods recipes from page 34 to get started.

Remember, babies are born with a sweet tooth. They will not develop a sweet tooth if you give them fruit early on. Include fruit purées as part of a varied diet.

Portioning & Meal Times

This is a portion guide to help you introduce food to your baby, based on starting to wean at 5½ months. Over this first stage, it's vital to use **4-6 month weaning pots** (30ml/1oz portion) for every meal. This is to ensure you don't affect the volume of your baby's milk intake, from which they gain essential nutrients. If you start earlier, complete the 14 days and continue with three 30ml/1oz meals each day, until 6 months of age.

DAY 1-3

meal 1: midday

texture: runny purée

first foods:
root vegetables

DAY 3-6

meal 1: breakfast
meal 2: midday

texture: runny purée

first foods:
root vegetables or ripe
fruit purées

DAY 6-9

meal 1: breakfast
meal 2: midday
meal 3: evening

texture: runny purée

mixed purées:
e.g. parsnip & apple

DAY 9-14

meal 1: breakfast
meal 2: midday
meal 3: evening

texture: runny purée

mixed purées:
e.g. carrot & cauliflower

Meal 1
Offer your baby their milk at 11am. Feed them a midday meal between 12 and 12:30pm. Make sure they are not too hungry as this is just a taste.

Meal 2
After about 3 days, if you feel your baby has taken well to the first few tastes, introduce a second meal at breakfast. It should be offered after baby's morning bottle, with a gap between the milk and food.

Meal 3
After a week, move your baby on to three meals a day. Their third meal can be given at about 5pm, after an afternoon milk feed at around 3pm. Be sure to increase the variety of purées offered to your baby.

Feeding your Baby

It's important to give your baby control when weaning so that they have a positive experience. It takes a little time for your baby to learn to take food from a spoon, and then figure out how to move it from the front of their tongue to the back of their mouth, so patience is key when getting started.

Giving control...

While offering your baby finger food ensures your baby has control, offering purées can also have the same outcome if you make sure to do the following:

Set the scene: Place a bowl with some of their food, a baby spoon and a beaker of water in front of them.

Enjoy the senses: Let your baby touch, explore and play with their food as they try to eat it. Meanwhile, you should have another bowl with most of the food. Spoon-feed them in between their attempts to self-feed.

Don't Clean: It's important not to clean your baby's hand or face whilst feeding no matter how much you're tempted to. Each mealtime needs to be a positive experience for your child. A sensory over-load of being constantly wiped can create a negative association with food.

If you follow this while weaning your baby you will have a messy but enjoyable weaning experience.

How to spoon feed...

1 For a baby starting to wean, fill the spoon a third of the way. If they've been feeding for a few weeks fill it half way up. Don't overfill the spoon as this may cause them to gag.

2 Tip your baby's lip with the spoon, allowing them to open their own mouth.

3 Rest the ball of the spoon on their tongue, making sure not to touch the top of their mouth. Try not to place the spoon too far back or they will gag.

4 Take the spoon out, again very gently. As you do this, the food will be at the front of their mouth, between their gums and lips. They will then guide the food around their mouth and crunch down (with their gums as no teeth are required). If you put the food on their tongue, they will be more likely to gag as this is where their gag reflex is at the early stages of weaning.

Tip: Use soft tipped spoons.

Preparation & Storage of food

It's important to prepare and store food correctly to ensure that your baby and family's food is safe to eat. Here is a quick and easy guide for you to follow:

Wash weaning pots with warm soapy water and air dry (there's no need to sterilise them).

Wash all fruits and vegetables with cold running water.

Label and date all foods you refrigerate or freeze. This will help you keep track of what food is inside and what needs to be used up first.

Fresh or home-made food should be stored for no longer than 72 hours (3 days) in the fridge. This will minimise bacteria growth.

Never wash chicken as it can contaminate water supplies and the kitchen sink.

To optimise nutrient retention and quality, use frozen foods within 3 months of freezing.

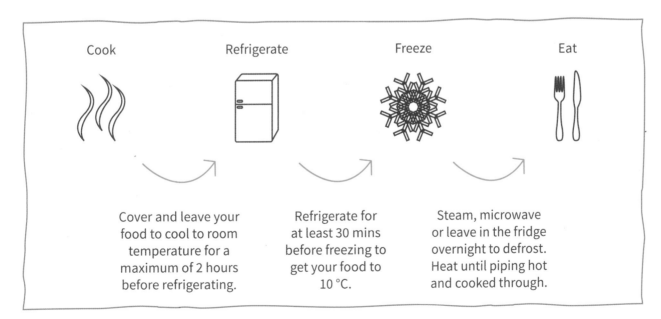

Cook

Refrigerate

Freeze

Eat

Cover and leave your food to cool to room temperature for a maximum of 2 hours before refrigerating.

Refrigerate for at least 30 mins before freezing to get your food to 10 °C.

Steam, microwave or leave in the fridge overnight to defrost. Heat until piping hot and cooked through.

Seasonal Calendar

— ••• —

Whether feeding baby or family, I like to follow the seasonal calendar. It's a really great way of introducing new fruits and vegetables. As well as being fresh and better tasting, seasonal produce is higher in nutritional value.

	Purée	Finger Food	Jan	Feb	Mar	Apr	May	Jun	Jul	Aug	Sep	Oct	Nov	Dec
Apples	Steam & purée	Grate or chop	●	●	●					●	●	●	●	●
Blackberries	Purée & strain if a first food	Cut in half							●	●	●			
Blueberries	Steam & purée	Cut in half							●	●	●			
Cherries	Stew gently & purée	Halve and de-stone							●	●				
Pears	Steam & purée	Offer ripe	●							●	●	●	●	●
Plums	Stew gently & purée	Offer ripe								●	●	●		
Raspberries	Add apple & purée	Offer as it is							●	●	●			
Rhubarb	Add apple or plum & purée	N/A	●	●	●									
Strawberries	Purée or mash & add to natural yogurt	Quarter					●	●	●	●				
Tomatoes	Roast with garlic & herbs	Quarter cherry tomatoes						●	●	●	●	●		

	Purée	Finger Food	Jan	Feb	Mar	Apr	May	Jun	Jul	Aug	Sep	Oct	Nov	Dec
Asparagus	Steam & purée	Steam/roast					X	X						
Beans	Steam, purée & add potato	Steam & chop							X	X	X			
Beetroot	Roast/steam & purée	Cook and grate or chop							X	X	X	X	X	X
Broccoli	Steam & purée	Steam florets									X			
Brussel Sprouts	Steam, purée & add peas	Cook and grate or chop	X	X								X	X	X
Cabbage	Steam, purée & add potato	Steam & shred	X	X	X	X	X	X	X	X	X	X	X	X
Carrots	Steam & purée	Steam & chop	X	X	X	X	X	X	X	X	X	X	X	X
Cauliflower	Steam & purée	Steam florets	X	X	X	X	X	X	X	X	X	X	X	X
Courgette	Steam & purée	Steam & chop							X	X	X	X		
Cucumber	Blend with yogurt	Chop to finger size pieces					X	X	X	X	X			
Kale	Steam, purée & add potato	Remove stalks & stems	X	X	X						X	X	X	X
Leeks	Sweat in oil/ butter & purée	Offer roasted	X	X	X						X	X	X	X
Parsnips	Steam & purée	Roast chunks	X								X	X	X	X
Peas	Steam & purée	Steam						X	X					
Peppers	Roast & purée	Raw								X	X	X		
Potatoes	Steam & mash	Roast chunks					X					X		
Spinach	Steam & purée	Steam, add unsalted butter	X	X	X	X	X	X	X	X	X	X		
Squash	Steam & purée	Roast wedges	X								X	X	X	X
Sweetcorn	Steam & purée	Steam									X			
Turnip	Steam & purée	Roast chunks							X	X	X	X	X	X

13

Moving on with Texture

From 6 months, begin to introduce more texture and variety into your baby's diet. Now is the time to start including baby in your family meals. The healthiest way to do this is to cook meals from scratch with good quality ingredients, without any added sugar or salt. I firmly believe that starting your baby early on family foods encourages them to accept a wider variety of foods and be less picky as they grow into a toddler. The recipes in this book are written with this in mind. Cook first for family and adapt for baby by puréeing or offering as a finger food.

Why Portion?

Having met many first time mothers in my weaning classes, I have learned that what stresses them out the most is how much to feed their baby. Portioning your baby's food during the weaning stages can really help to calm parents, and it can help ensure success during the weaning journey.

Milk Intake
It is especially important to portion your baby's food before six months to ensure your baby's milk intake isn't reduced. Feeding them more than they need can cause them to be too full for milk.

Healthy Habits
By portioning your baby's food from the start, you are more likely to continue healthy portion control as they grow up. It is just as important to portion food for your toddler and child.

More Variety
If your baby is still hungry after their portion of food, you can offer a finger food or a healthy dessert which differs from the meal they just had. This increases the variety of foods in your baby's diet.

A Guide for Parents
Portioning will help you to understand what to feed your baby, and how much, based on their age.

Reduce Waste
Your time is precious, and so are your home cooked meals. Storing leftovers or batch cooked meals in portions will ensure you only remove what you actually need from the freezer.

Portioning from 6-12 months...

Try out my delicious recipes for baby and family from *page 76*.

| 60ml/2oz | 90ml/3oz | 120ml/4oz | 180ml/6oz |

6-7 MONTHS

3 meals

texture: smooth and slightly thicker purée, no lumps

introduce: dairy, fish, gluten, grains, meat soft finger foods and a beaker of water

7-8 MONTHS

3 meals

texture: thicker purée with increased texture

introduce: increased variety of finger foods - add dips such as unsalted nut butter

8-9 MONTHS

3 meals

texture: minced and mashed with soft lumps

introduce: stronger flavours e.g. oily fish such as salmon

9-12 MONTHS

3 meals

texture: minced and finely chopped

introduce: increased texture, finger foods and 1 or 2 snacks a day

At 6 months your baby is most accepting of new tastes and textures, so it's really important to take advantage of this window of opportunity.

Increasing texture from 6 months is key, so that your baby will accept a variety of foods. Remember, if your baby rejects a food, it may be the texture and not that they dislike the taste. Try puréeing it further or wait a week before offering it again.

Introducing...

...

Here's how to introduce key food groups to your baby's diet.

Gluten

What is gluten?

Gluten is a protein found in crops such as wheat, rye and barley. Oats can also be exposed to this protein during the production process. As such, any foods from flour and cereals, to breads, crackers, pasta and many sauces (pasta sauces, BBQ etc.) contain gluten.

When to introduce

Introduce gluten between 6 and 12 months of age but *not before 4 months*. Delaying beyond this can increase your weaning baby's risk of developing coeliac disease and diabetes in later childhood. Introduce foods containing gluten slowly, allowing a few days between feeds to monitor any possible reactions. Be extra vigilant if you have a history of coeliac disease in your family.

How to introduce

Week 1
1 portion of foods containing gluten once every 3 days.
e.g. ½ a weetabix with warm full fat cows milk

Week 2
1 portion of foods containing gluten once every 2 days.
e.g. Biscotti with Babycinno (pg 183)

Week 3
1 portion of foods containing gluten every day.
e.g. Chicken Parmigiana (pg 86)

Subsequently, you can include foods containing gluten in every meal, if you wish.

Always talk to a doctor if you have any concerns about introducing any food groups to your baby.

Meat, Poultry & Fish

Benefits

Meat, poultry and fish are a great source of protein, vitamins and minerals, all of which your baby needs for growth and development.

When to introduce

As soon as your baby can handle some texture, you can start to introduce meat, poultry & fish. It is advisable to introduce them from *6 months of age*. If you wait any longer your baby may reject them as they have a very different texture to fruit and vegetable purées.

How to introduce

When your baby is accepting of food from a spoon, well-cooked soft meat can then be puréed and mixed with vegetables. My Baby's First Chicken Purée is great to get started *(pg 53)*.

When your baby is better able for finger foods, offer meat in cubes or slices.

Foods to avoid before 12 months

Honey - Bacteria commonly found in honey can cause infant botulism.
Added sugar - Sugar has little nutrition and contributes to tooth decay.
Added salt - Babies and young children's kidneys cannot cope with excess salt. See *page 29* for more info.
Raw/undercooked eggs - Salmonella bacteria in raw and undercooked eggs may cause food poisoning.*
Raw shellfish - This can cause food poisioning and is best avoided.

*Advice is changing on this. In the UK, as long as an egg has the British Lion mark, your baby can have runny eggs from 6 months.

Dairy

What is dairy?

Dairy products include cow's milk, cheese and yoghurt. Dairy is essential for your child, as it is packed full of nutrients, such as calcium, that support healthy growth of your baby's bones.

Dairy as a Healthy Snack

While it is best to introduce dairy early on, it should not be your "go-to" snack. It should be offered, like everything else, in moderation. Try to avoid more than 2-3 servings a day.

Is Low Fat Better?

It is best not to choose low fat dairy products. Full fat is best, as it is less processed. Low fat products are generally high in salt or sugar to make up for the lost flavour. Fat is essential for the healthy brain development of your baby. It is not advised to introduce low or reduced fat dairy products to your child until the age of 3, unless otherwise instructed by your doctor.

When to introduce

Offering cow's milk as a main drink before 12 months is not recommended. Your baby should drink breast or formula milk until 12 months. However, if a recipe calls for milk, you should use cow's milk. As long as your baby is getting their recommended daily intake of breast or formula milk, you can include cow's milk in your baby's meals, for example in porridge or my Fish Pies *(pg 114)*.

Dairy products, such as plain natural yoghurt and full fat mild cheeses, are great for baby.

How to introduce

Yoghurt

Stir some yoghurt into your baby's cereal or offer as a snack topped with your own home-made fruit purées. Opt for plain natural yoghurt. Flavoured, low fat and branded kinds are usually high in sugar.

Cheese

Cheese is a great finger food for your baby served cut into strips or cubes. Start with milder cheeses; Cheddar and cottage cheeses are good first options. If your baby struggles to grasp the cubes or slices, try melting it over steamed vegetables or in my tasty Broccoli Tots *(pg 150)*. Avoid cheeses made with unpasterised or raw milk, as they are not suitable for a babies immune system.

Allergies & Substitutes

A few foods are considered highly allergenic, such as peanuts, eggs, cow's milk, wheat, gluten and shellfish. Generally avoid these only if you or your partner has an allergy (not an intolerance) to the food. For everyone else, introduce these foods from 6 months of age. Look out for any signs of an allergic reaction. Seek advice from a healthcare provider if you have any concerns.

There are lots of **milk** substitutes such as oat, nut and rice milks.

You can buy dairy-free **cheese** substitutes made from nut milk. For sandwiches you can use ripe avocados instead.

Get dairy-free nut-based yoghurt. For allergies to cow's milk, goat milk yoghurt is also available.

To replace 1 egg: Mix in 1 tbsp of ground flaxseed with 2½ tbsp of water. Leave to sit for 5 minutes to thicken.

For **butter**, substitute with a nut butter, vegetable spread or olive oil.

Coconut flour, almond flour, oat flour and rice flour are wheat & gluten free **flours**.

Introducing Finger Foods

Most of my recipes can be given to your baby as a finger food from 6 months. Simply serve unblended so your baby can grab the food with their hands. Make sure to chop any pieces of meat into pea size pieces. Serve at least one meal a day as a finger food with a dip and dipper to increase variety. Keep in mind, your baby is more likely to accept finger food if they're not too full from already eating a purée. Some children don't like being fed, so finger food is a great way of giving them control of their meals. Take your baby's lead! If they prefer to feed themselves, let them do so.

How to know your baby is ready?

1 Your baby should be able to sit upright unaided.

2 They'll be developing their pincer grasp (the ability to hold objects between their forefinger and thumb). They may not fully master this until 7 months, but you should familiarise them with finger foods at an early stage so that it is not alien to them. While developing the pincer grasp, they may use their whole hand to pick things up by clasping the item in their palms. At the start, it is best to place the food into their hand, and let your baby bring it to their own mouth.

3 Your baby should be starting to chew at this stage, using their gums to mash foods. (Teeth aren't necessary to chew.)

Tip: Be sure to cook your baby's portion a little longer than yours, to ensure it is soft enough for them to enjoy.

Start off offering food in the shape of a finger, placing it in the palm of your baby's hand. Then gradually move on to pea size pieces when your baby has developed their pincer grasp.
My Roasted Sweet Potato Fingers recipe on *page 142* is the perfect first finger food.

How to introduce Finger Foods...

1 Offer foods that are easy to hold. Begin with finger size pieces and move onto pea size bites, as soon as they develop their pincer grab.
2 Make sure to offer foods that can be squashed between your index finger and thumb. This ensures that your baby's gums will be able to chew it.
3 Don't put food into your baby's mouth. You need to give your baby full control when offering finger food.
4 Do not force, or let them force, food into their mouths.
5 Adapt meals to be offered as finger food. Use less sauce or large pasta shapes so that your baby can pick up the food.
6 Try to offer a dip along with the finger food to increase variety.

Dippers...

Fruit & Vegetables

• Soft cooked vegetables such as green beans, parsnip or carrots
• Roasted Sweet Potato Fingers *(pg 142)*
• Small, soft pieces of fruit such as banana, pear, apple, peach, nectarine or mango
• Soft cooked baby sweetcorn, sugar snap peas or mangetout
• Soft cooked florets of broccoli
• Soft cooked slices of butternut squash

Breads & Pasta

• Fingers of toasted bread
• Well cooked pasta shapes such as fusilli
• Breadsticks

Cheese

• Sticks of firm cheese such as Cheddar

Meat & Poultry

• Strips of cooked meat or poultry such as beef, lamb, chicken, turkey or pork

Dips...

• Homemade Hummus 3 Ways *(pg 164)*
• Homemade Pestos *(pg 163)*
• Cheese spread
• Smooth nut butter
• Homemade Tomato Sauce *(pg 137)*

Gagging & Choking

When introducing food to your baby, it's normal to be anxious. Naturally, parents will worry about their child gagging or choking on solid foods. It's important not to let this fear keep you from offering finger foods or more textured foods to your baby. It can be easy to get confused between gagging and choking, so it's important to know the difference between the two.

Gagging...

Gagging is a safety reflex that prevents choking. It's caused when a baby puts too much food in their mouth, or, if a food is too far back in their mouth. Babies are born with their gag reflex at the tip of the tongue, so it's likely they will gag at some point when feeding.

Key Signs:

- Your child may open their mouth and thrust their tongue forward. (Their face may turn red)
- They may sputter and/or cough.
- They may display looks of discomfort rather than fear/terror.

Gagging is a normal part of learning how to eat. It should be seen as a positive reaction. Your baby is simply pushing food forward so that they don't choke. Just remember, they are not spitting out food because they don't like it. Rather, they are getting used to a new texture on their tongue.

Choking...

Choking occurs when a person's airways are blocked. It is understandable to be worried about your baby choking, but you should not let that fear stop you from weaning your baby once they are ready, or from introducing finger food and foods with more texture.

Key Signs:

- Your child's face will turn blue.
- They may go silent and/or show an inability to make noise. (However, soft or high pitched sounds may be heard while inhaling).
- Your child may begin coughing (in an attempt to clear the passage). This can be normal, or weak/ineffective should they fail to clear the passage.

In the rare case that your child is choking, you may need to do back blows or chest thrusts to dislodge the blockage. Always seek immediate medical assistance from the emergency services or a qualified first aider.

How to prevent choking...

There are a few essential tips you can follow to prevent choking:

1 Sit your baby upright when eating. Don't allow them to eat when crawling, walking or distracted.
2 Don't leave your baby unattended or without supervision while eating.
3 Do not force, or let them force, food into their mouths.
4 Do not attempt to interrupt the gagging process. This can lead to choking and panic.
5 Avoid foods that are a choking hazard. Small, firm and round foods should not be given to babies or small children. Other choking hazards include bones from fish or meat.
6 Know the difference between gagging and choking.

Refusing to eat

As a parent, it can be frustrating when your baby is not interested in, or refuses to eat, their meal. This is particularly difficult when your baby initially eats all their food and then suddenly stops. Watching your baby throw food on the floor can be disheartening when you have put so much time and effort into preparing healthy, homemade meals. When this happens you should avoid forcing food and simply move onto the next meal. It is important to remember that during the first year you are just teaching a baby to eat solid food. Food rejections can occur for a number of reasons:

Stomach capacity...

Babies and young children have a much smaller stomach capacity than adults. Therefore, the amount of foods and fluids they can manage is smaller. If a child fills up on fluids or snacks, they will be less likely to eat at meal-times. By offering the right foods and less fluids (other than your baby's milk), you can ensure that the small amounts that your child eats will have the right nutrients for healthy growth and wellness. Stick to our portion guide on feeding your child (*pg 9* and *pg 15*).

Things that may affect appetite
- Not allowing enough time between milk feeds and weaning food.
- Breast milk or formula; stick to the guidelines on milk intake for a weaning baby.
- Continuously snacking throughout the day.

Not accepting the spoon...

Some babies do not like being offered a spoon. It may be that the spoon is too hard or too wide. Offer spoons that are narrow and a little soft tipped. If this fails, your baby may not want to be spoon-fed and this is fine!

Instead, they may be more accepting of finger foods where they have full control and can self-feed (*pg 20-21*).

Overfeeding...

It is important not to feed your baby every time they cry. Your baby needs time to develop a hunger for meals, and so should not be fed every time they feel peckish. Without this sense of hunger or appetite developing from an early stage in weaning, it may be difficult to encourage your child to eat at mealtimes during their toddler stage.

Let your baby eat according to their appetite; a bottle or weaning meal doesn't have to be finished every time. If they are able to register that they are full and stop feeding on their own, it is a good sign.

Teething...

Teething can cause discomfort in many forms for your little one. When that happens, it is normal that they don't want to eat. Teething can start as early as 4 months, and can disrupt feeding patterns. However, don't be discouraged! Simply offer cold foods such as a fruit purée or yoghurt. Unsweetened teething biscuits are also great for baby to gnaw on. My biscotti recipe on *page 183* is perfect to help soothe your little one's teething pain.

Tired...

Sometimes, a lack of appetite may just mean your child is too tired to eat. Ensure you are not compromising nap times during the day to fit in feeds. Work to a schedule that suits your baby; should they need a nap at a certain time each day, stick to it and work in feeds around that. If it happens that your baby is having an off day in terms of sleep and appetite, offer a meal with something familiar that they enjoy to make the feed less stressful.

Fussy Eaters - 1 year+

Every child will go through a fussy or picky stage where they reject foods that they used to eat, or only want food shaped a certain way. As a busy parent, it can be frustrating trying to keep up with ever-changing likes and dislikes. If you have a child that is starting to become a little fussy, remember that this is just a phase they are going through called 'neophobia'; a fear of new things. It's how you, as a parent, deal with it that determines the outcome. I have listed a few steps that you can take when your baby/toddler starts to become picky with their food.

Never offer alternatives

If you offer alternatives, your child will learn that if they reject their food, they will be given another option. Alternatives can come in different forms, whether you offer a more puréed version of a meal if baby rejects texture or if you reach for a yoghurt if they refuse their meal. Remember your child will eat if they are hungry.

Eat together as a family

Lead the way. Sitting down as a family is a great way to teach your child about food. If spoon-feeding your child, make sure to eat your own meal first and then help your child. It's important that we don't stop enjoying mealtimes. For your weaning baby, offer them some finger foods so everybody can enjoy the meal together and at the same time.

Only allow 20 minutes per meal

This is as much for your own sanity as it is for the child. Let your toddler know that they only have 20 minutes to finish the meal and then remove the food when the time is up. If you can place the food back into the fridge, I guarantee as soon as their tummy starts to rumble, they will be back looking for it. What has actually happened is that the anxiety that they felt when they first came to the table is now gone and the hunger has returned.

Comfortable food with uncomfortable food

This is a great way of introducing new, unfamiliar foods to your child, whether you want to broaden their palate or reintroduce foods they ate during the weaning stages. For example, the comfortable food may be chicken and the uncomfortable food may be carrots. When it comes to vegetables, offering 2 or 3 options will help them feel like they have a choice. Remember to try to mix up the vegetables that are on offer each day.

Remove uncomfortable food

When a child is upset about the food in front of them, it can be tempting to take it away. Instead place it in a bowl beside them and make sure to praise your child for leaving it there. Once they are open to tasting the food they should recognise it from the weaning stages and eventually go on to including it in their meals again. When removing foods from the table it may take up to 22 times to get it back on their plate. By placing it in a bowl beside them this time will be reduced.

Portion Plates

A portion or separation plate is also a great idea when you are feeding a picky or fussy toddler. It can reduce anxiety at the table because uncomfortable foods will not be touching comfortable ones.

Get your children into the kitchen

As well as showing your children a love of food it can help break down any fear they have around certain ingredients. A child that helps prepare food is much more likely to accept it.

Limit snacks

You should only provide two snacks throughout the day. One mid-morning and one mid-afternoon. Make sure there is at least a 2 hour gap between snacks and your child's meal. Offer your child a snack no later then 3pm and then sit down for dinner at 5 or 5:30pm.

Limit milk intake

As soon as your child is one year's of age they will move onto drinking cow's milk. If you find they are filling up on milk before their meal offer water as part of their meal and then offer the milk after the meal.

The Importance of Iron...

Iron is important in your growing child's diet to maintain healthy blood and normal growth and development. Most babies are born with stores of iron that last about six months. After this, your growing child needs to get iron from the foods that he or she eats. If your child is not getting enough iron they might seem:

• Tired and pale with a poor appetite.
• Less able to fight infection.

What are the best sources of iron?

• Red meat, such as beef and lamb, is the best source of iron. Poultry and pork are also good.

• Eggs, peas, beans, lentils, green leafy vegetables, such as spinach and broccoli, are also a great source.

Eating foods rich in vitamin C at the same time improves iron absorption. Fresh fruit and vegetables are good sources of vitamin C.

Reading Labels

Knowing what foods are healthy options for our children is not always as straightforward as it may seem. As a parent, it is essential that you learn how to read food labels correctly. Then, when you need to make a quick decision while standing in the supermarket queue, you will be well-equipped to do so. Here is the breakdown of fats, salt and sugar to make it clear what to look for. Always look at per 100g rather than per portion.

Food...

	Good	Bad
Total Fat	Less than 3g per 100g	Over 20g per 100g
Saturated Fat	Less than 1.5g per 100g	Over 5g per 100g
Sugar	Less than 5g per 100g	Over 10g per 100g
Salt	Less than 0.3g per 100g	Over 1.3g per 100g

Tip:

Take a photo of these tables to help make your next shop easier.

Drink...

	Good	Bad
Total Fat	Less than 1.5g per 100g	Over 10g per 100g
Saturated Fat	Less than 0.75g per 100g	Over 2.5g per 100g
Sugar	Less than 2.5g per 100g	Over 7.5g per 100g
Salt	Less than 0.15g per 100g	Over 0.75g per 100g

Salt...

Salt is addictive and hard for our kidneys to handle in excessive amounts. If you are preparing homemade food, there should be no issue with salt. It's when you start to introduce snacks that you will need to read labels. When you see labels with sodium levels rather then salt, just multiply the sodium level by 2.5 to get the salt level.

Age	Safe Daily Amount	Sodium Equivalent
6-12 months	No more than 1g	0.4g
1-3 years	No more than 2g	0.8g
4-6 years	No more than 3g	1.2g
7-11 years	No more than 5g	2.0g
11 years+	No more than 6g	2.4g

Don't forget, when cooking with stock cubes that they contain salt. Always use low salt versions or prepare your own.

Check out *page 31*

Cereals...

The majority of children's breakfast cereals contain more sugar then other cereals, so it is best to avoid them. For a weaning baby avoid any cereals that are too high in sugar or fibre (All Bran, etc.) and avoid muesli, which may contain whole or chopped nuts.

	Good	Bad
Sugar	Less than 5g per 100g	Over 10g per 100g
Salt	Less than 0.3g per 100g	Over 1.3 per 100g

Healthy choices:

Weetabix
Ready Brek
Oatibix
Shredded Wheat
Porridge

Batch Cooking

———— ··· ————

As a busy Mum, I don't believe that I could offer a healthy home cooked meal night after night if it wasn't for batch cooking. I have a few 20 minute meals that I prepare when I get home from work, but there are busier days where I take out my bolognese or chilli from the freezer. If you are organised, you should never have to reach for shop bought alternatives that are not healthy for the family and not suitable for baby.

1. Choose your recipes wisely

Decide on the four or five recipes you're going to make in one session and do one big shop for all the ingredients. Double check you have the spices and tinned goods you require. Don't reinvent the wheel when it comes to freezer meals. Prepare meals you are familiar with, and ones that your family love. Stews, soups and casseroles are classic freezer friendly dishes. Try my Chilli Con Carne on *page 93,* for the perfect batch cooking meal .

2. Have enough storage pots to portion your food for the entire family

Having the right storage pots on hand will make your cooking more efficient and less stressful. Portioning your batch cook will make sure everyone is eating the correct amounts of food. It will also prevent wasting your valuable cooking.

Check out **MummyCooks.com** for my portion pots.

3. Use your food processor

Don't bother hand chopping 6 onions and 2 heads of garlic – you will never want to batch cook again! Instead, use your food processor to help whenever you can. This is also ideal for sauces and purées. Just make sure to use the 'pulse mode' rather then blending.

4. Double up

Don't be afraid to double up on your recipes. My bolognese is perfect to batch cook and can be used for a lasagne or simply serve with spaghetti *(pg 99)*.

5. Watch the vegetables

For some recipes, such as soups and stews, aim to under cook your vegetables slightly. They will get a second round of cooking when preparing the meal at a later stage. This will ensure freshness and also prevent them from becoming mushy!

6. Cool foods fully

Let all dishes come to room temperature for no more than 2 hours. Place in the fridge for around ½ an hour before freezing. When defrosting, transfer your food to the fridge overnight, or heat it directly in the container; never let food defrost on the counter top!

7. Label all your food

Label your batch cooking to help you keep track of what food you have stored. Use my easy peel labels so that you can reuse your portion pots and easily re-label them for your latest batch cook.

8. Use up within 3 to 4 months

Make sure to use your food up within 3 months. Rearrange your freezer once a month and position the foods that need to be used up first to the front of your freezer. This will avoid any waste and also remind you of what you have stored away.

Using Stock Cubes

Homemade stock is by far the best and will give your cooking a wonderful wholesome flavour. However, It can be very difficult to find the time to make your own stock. This is where low salt stock cubes are a great substitute!

Using stock in your baby and family's food will make purées, soups, stews, curries and risottos taste much better. There are no stock cubes on the market that contain zero salt, so for baby make sure to always look for low salt versions.

Don't be afraid to add stock to your baby's food. When you consider how much your little one actually eats, a pinch of salt to your baby's diet will do no harm, as long as you stick to the recommended guidelines *(pg 29)*.

As your baby grows and eats more adult foods, the intake of salt may also increase. To limit this, avoid processed foods as much as possible as they are often very high in salt. Homemade food is the best, as you can control how much salt you put in.

Get started with stock cubes by trying out my Butternut Squash and Lentil Purée *(pg 48)* or Lamb Curry *(pg 94)*.

How to use the Recipes

Everything you will need to see you through your baby's entire weaning journey.

Freezer guide

When freezing your food, it is recommended that you use it within 3 to 4 months. However, keep in mind when preparing food for a 6 month old, the texture may not be relevant for a 9 month old. So, in the early stages it is best to keep your batch cooking to a minimum. Alternatively you can freeze your food without blending and then blend to the desired consistency after you defrost it.

Portion Sizes for Family

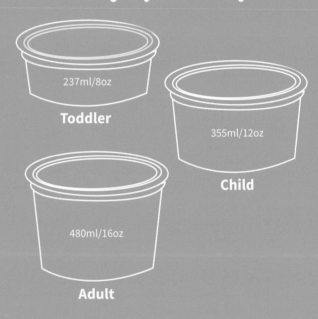

237ml/8oz
Toddler

355ml/12oz
Child

480ml/16oz
Adult

Portion Sizes for Baby

30ml/1oz
4-6m

60ml/2oz
6-7m

90ml/3oz
7-8m

120ml/4oz
8-9m

180ml/6oz
9-12m

First food recipes are given in portion sizes based on the texture and consistency of the food as follows:

4-6m - Blended to a runny purée
6-7m - Smooth and slightly thicker purée, no lumps
7-8m - Thicker purée with increased texture
8-9m - Minced and mashed with soft lumps
9-12m - Minced and finely chopped

Move from First Foods to Baby & Family Foods

The recipes in the First Foods section of this book suit a baby starting off on their weaning journey. They can easily be blended down so that there is little or no texture. As your baby gets used to some texture, you can start on family foods and adapt them for baby. This is why the next section includes a range of recipes that are for both family and baby. Simply blend to your baby's desired consistency. Do not blend white potato or pasta, as they do not blend well. Adapting family foods and feeding them to your baby from an early age will ensure your baby has an easy transition to family meals from 12 months of age.

Finger Food or Baby-Led Weaning

All my Baby & Family Meal recipes can be served as a finger food. Meat can be removed from a main dish and served finely chopped or in slices. Vegetables should be nice and soft, so that they can be squished between your thumb and finger. Serve up dips with dippers, such as roasted vegetables with sauces, to increase variety. See page 20 for more advice on finger foods.

Batch Cooking

Always think about doubling your quantities when cooking for the family. The best way to batch cook is to chop your vegetables in a blender. Make sure to use the pulse button when chopping onions or celery or it will turn into mush.

Muffin Recipes

I have included a variety of muffin recipes, both sweet and savoury. I have suggested greasing or lining a muffin tin, but my best recommendation is to invest in a silicone muffin case. You don't have to grease or line it, the muffins are so easy to remove, and it's also easy to clean.

Mix things Up

The recipes in this book are not exhaustive. Change things up by using seasonal fruits and vegetables.

First Foods

Always try to steam your baby's fruit and vegetables to retain the most nutrients. Cook them for a little longer then you would prepare for yourself and blend with some of the cooking water or your baby's milk.

If you are starting to wean your baby before 6 months, it is important to first introduce runny purées so that your baby will accept solid foods. It is also important to start progressing on with texture as soon as your baby will allow. Begin with my single purée recipes and move onto mixing purées so that by six months your baby is eating three meals a day. Then, you can add variety and include meat, fish and grains.

Baby's First Purées

First Foods

Get your baby started with root vegetable and fruit purées such as butternut squash, sweet potato, carrot, pear or apple. Remember, everyday ingredients for adults such as broccoli, carrots, apples and pears will appear strong in flavour to baby. This is why I recommend beginning with single ingredient purées and then moving along to combination purées once your baby has had time to adapt.

Your baby is born with a sweet tooth so will be more accepting of sweeter vegetables such as carrots, sweet potato and butternut squash.

1 Peel, wash and chop your fruit or vegetable.

2 Steam until tender and cooked through.

3 Blend with cooking water, breast or formula milk to form a runny purée.

4 Store portions in your weaning pots and freeze extras for future use.

4-6 months – Blended to a runny purée
6-7 months - Smooth and slightly thicker purée, no lumps
7-8 months - Thicker purée with increased texture
8-9 months - Minced and mashed with soft lumps
9-12 months – Minced and finely chopped

Alternatively you can bake a whole butternut squash or sweet potato in an oven, then purée.

 FREEZER FRIENDLY

PERFECT FOR TUMMIES 4 MONTHS+

Beetroot & Blueberry Purée

Making the most of seasonal produce ensures your little one gets a variety of nutrients to boost their immune system. Beetroot are in season from July to December and blueberries are in season from July to October. Your baby will love this recipe packed full of vitamin C. The sweetness of the blueberries will encourage your baby to be accepting of the earthy flavours from the beetroot.

Portions: 6 x 30ml/1oz

2 medium beetroot
100g blueberries fresh/frozen

> Introduce vibrant and colourful foods to your baby so that they are more accepting of a variety of foods when a toddler.

1 Rinse the blueberries and beetroot with water and remove the beetroot skin with a grater.

2 Cube the beetroot and place in a medium saucepan, along with the blueberries.

3 Add just enough water to cover the tops of the beetroot and blueberries. Cook on a medium high heat for 10-15 minutes, until the beetroot are tender.

4 Pour into a blender and blend until smooth.

5 Store portions in your weaning pots and freeze extras for future use.

 FREEZER FRIENDLY

PERFECT FOR TUMMIES | 4 MONTHS+

Asparagus & Apple

—— ••• ——

By combining sweet with savoury, your baby is more likely to accept new tastes such as asparagus.

Portions: 6 x 30ml/1oz

1 apple
Handful of asparagus

1   Wash, peel and cube the apple and asparagus.

2   Place the apple and asparagus in a steamer and cook for 10-15 minutes, until tender and cooked through.

3   Blend or mash, adding cooking water, if needed, to desired consistency.

Avocado & Banana

—— ••• ——

Banana combined with the healthy fats from the avocado makes for a creamy sweet treat that your weaning baby will love! It's perfect to whip up on the go - just carry a banana and avocado with you when you're out and about.

Portions: 6 x 30ml/1oz

1 ripe banana (sweeter if ripe)
1 avocado, cut in half and pitted

1   Peel the banana and mash with a fork in a bowl.

2   Spoon out the avocado flesh and add to the bowl.

3   Mash together until mixed well.

Parsnip & Pear

———— ••• ————

This is the perfect combination to make the earthy flavours of parsnip more palatable for your baby.

Portions: 6 x 30ml/1oz

1 parsnip, peeled and chopped
1 pear, peeled and chopped

1 Add the chopped parsnip and pear to a steamer and cook for 10-15 minutes until tender.

2 Blend or mash, adding cooking water, if needed, to desired consistency.

Peach, Raspberry & Quinoa

———— ••• ————

The combination of naturally sweet fruit and protein rich quinoa makes this a delicious and nutritious meal that your baby will be sure to love.

Portions: 6 x 30ml/1oz

1 ripe peach, peeled and chopped
90g raspberries
100g quinoa

1 Add the quinoa and water to a saucepan and bring to the boil. Reduce the heat and add the peach. Simmer for 10 minutes. Add the raspberries, and cook for 5 minutes further, until the quinoa is cooked.

2 Mash and serve as is or blend for a younger baby.

Peach Purée with Ginger & Basil

First Foods

Make the most of naturally sweet peaches and whip up some of this delicious purée with a twist. The infusion of basil and ginger will be sure to get your little one's taste buds tingling. It's also delicious drizzled over pancakes. Use this purée as a dip for pancakes to mix textures together once your little one is 6 months and ready for finger food.

Portions: 6 x 30ml/1oz

2 peaches, peeled and chopped
1 tbsp freshly grated ginger
1 tbsp finely chopped basil
Fresh lemon juice

1 In a small saucepan place the peaches, ginger, basil and fresh lemon juice.

2 Drizzle with a little water and bring to the boil ever so briefly.

3 Lower to a simmer for about 5 minutes.

4 Place contents into a blender and blend until you get the desired consistency.

5 Store portions in your weaning pots and freeze extras for future use.

This purée is packed full of vitamin C making it perfect to boost your baby's immune system if they have a cold.

 FREEZER FRIENDLY

PERFECT FOR TUMMIES 4 MONTHS+

Apple, Cinnamon & Prune Purée

This recipe always goes down a treat in my Mummy Cooks weaning class. It's also perfect to help babies if they become constipated, which can often happen as you introduce foods into their diet. Given the slightly textured nature of this purée, it is best to delay feeding this until 1 or 2 weeks after commencing the weaning process. When your baby is a little older, have it as a dessert with some natural yoghurt.

Portions: 6 x 60ml/2oz

3 red apples
9 prunes
Cinnamon
Natural full fat yoghurt (optional)

1 Preheat the oven to 180°C.

2 Wash and core the apples. If you don't have an apple corer, use a knife to cut out the centre, starting at the stem and working your way down.

3 Stuff 3 pitted prunes inside each apple and sprinkle a little cinnamon on top.

4 Cover with foil and bake in the oven for 30-40 minutes or until the apples are very soft.

5 Remove from the oven and place in a blender. Blend to your desired consistency. Add water to make a runny purée.

6 Store portions in your weaning pots and freeze extras for future use.

Cinnamon adds great flavour and is also a natural pain reliever. Perfect for a teething baby!

 FREEZER FRIENDLY

PERFECT FOR TUMMIES 4 MONTHS+

Butternut Squash & Apple Purée

This is a lovely simple recipe that allows you to cook the butternut squash without having to peel it. Squash is a wonderful first food for your baby and is high in vitamins and calcium.

Portions: 9 x 60ml/2oz

1 butternut squash
2 red apples
Pinch of cinnamon

Try this out with brown rice - blend for a smaller baby.

1   Preheat the oven to 180°C.

2   Prepare your butternut squash by cutting it in half and scooping out the seeds.

3   Place the butternut squash halves face up on a roasting tray.

4   Peel and cube your apples and place inside the butternut squash where the seeds were. Sprinkle with cinnamon.

5   Roast in the oven for 40 minutes or until the skin puckers and the flesh feels soft.

6   Scoop out the squash and apples, and blend as needed, adding water to thin if required. You may also chop or dice and serve them up as a finger food.

7   Store portions in your weaning pots and freeze extras for future use.

❄ FREEZER FRIENDLY   PERFECT FOR TUMMIES | 4 MONTHS+

Courgette, Pea & Mint Purée

First Foods

This courgette and pea purée infused with mint is a great way to introduce a variety of flavours to your weaning baby.

Portions: 6 x 60ml/2oz

2 courgettes
Large handful of peas
1 tbsp mint leaves, finely chopped

1 Slice the courgette into chunks and place in a steamer along with the peas.

2 Sprinkle in the mint and cook for 10-15 minutes, until the courgette is tender and cooked.

3 Blend or mash. Add cooking water if it is not runny enough.

4 Store portions in your weaning pots and freeze extras for future use.

> Adding herbs to your baby's food introduces new flavours and textures to their meal. Herbs are also packed full of immune boosting nutrients.

 FREEZER FRIENDLY

PERFECT FOR TUMMIES | 4 MONTHS+

Butternut Squash & Lentil Purée

First Foods

This recipe is full of flavour and is a real crowd pleaser in my weaning classes. Add extra stock to make it into a delicious soup for the entire family!

Portions: 5 x 90ml/3oz

250g butternut squash
50g red lentils
Low salt vegetable stock (enough to cover)

1 Peel, de-seed and cube your squash.

2 Place your cubed squash into a small saucepan with the lentils and add enough stock to just cover everything.

3 Bring to a simmer and cook uncovered for 20 minutes or until the butternut squash and lentils are soft.

4 When cooked, blend to your desired consistency. Add more stock if making into a soup.

5 Store portions in your weaning pots and freeze extras for future use.

> Soak your lentils for about 30 minutes before cooking. This makes them easier for your baby to digest.

 FREEZER FRIENDLY

PERFECT FOR TUMMIES | 4 MONTHS+

Broccoli, Pear & Tahini Purée

First Foods

The addition of tahini to broccoli and pear makes for a delicious creamy taste your baby is sure to love!

Portions: 10 x 90ml/3oz

1 head of broccoli
2 pears
3 tbsp of tahini

Tahini is made from sesame seeds: avoid if you or your partner has an allergy to nuts. (Sesame seeds are not considered to be nuts, but certain proteins in sesame seeds can trigger allergy symptoms similar to a nut allergy.)

1 Prepare your steamer. Wash the broccoli and separate into florets. Add to the steamer.

2 Peel and chop the pears into chunks. Add the pear to the broccoli in the steamer and cook for 10-15 minutes.

3 Once tender and cooked through, remove from the heat. Add the tahini.

4 Blend or mash to your desired consistency, adding water to make it runny.

5 Store portions in your weaning pots and freeze extras for future use.

 FREEZER FRIENDLY

PERFECT FOR TUMMIES | 4 MONTHS+

Brussels Sprout & Pea Purée

Brussels sprouts are a vegetable children love to hate. However, if you introduce it early in the weaning stages your baby is more likely to accept the taste and texture of it.

Portions: 6 x 60ml/2oz

15 small Brussels sprouts
100g peas, fresh or frozen
3 sprigs flat leaf parsley, chopped

Brussels sprouts are in season during winter and spring. Buy them at these times as they're fresh and taste better. Choose smaller sprouts, as larger ones can be bitter and unpleasant for your baby.

1 Remove the outer leaves from the sprouts and cut off the base.

2 Prepare your steamer and add the sprouts.

3 After about 10 minutes, add the peas and parsley and cook until just tender.

4 Drain and pulse the vegetables in a food processor until smooth. Add cooking water to help blend, if needed.

5 Store portions in your weaning pots and freeze extras for future use.

 FREEZER FRIENDLY

PERFECT FOR TUMMIES | 4 MONTHS+

Salmon & Sweet Potato Purée

---•••---

First Foods

It is important to introduce fish to your weaning baby early on to allow them to develop a taste for it. This salmon and sweet potato recipe is a great way to introduce stronger tasting fish. It can be served as a purée, or mashed to dip with finger foods such as pitta bread or toast slices.

Portions: 6 x 90ml/3oz

350ml low salt vegetable stock
150g frozen peas
1 large sweet potato, peeled and cubed
2 salmon fillets

Always flake fish before blending to make sure it does not contain any bones.

1 Place a large saucepan over a medium heat and add the stock. Bring to the boil, then add the vegetables.

2 Lower the heat to a simmer for 15-20 minutes. Once the sweet potato has begun to soften, add the salmon to the saucepan.

3 Cover and allow the salmon to poach for about 8-10 minutes. Remove the salmon and flake into a large bowl, ensuring there are no small bones.

4 Put the vegetables into a blender and blend.

5 Portion the vegetables into your pots and add the fish on top. Alternatively, you can blend the salmon if your baby is not used to texture.

6 Freeze extra portions for future use.

❄ FREEZER FRIENDLY

PERFECT FOR TUMMIES | 6 MONTHS+

Baby's First Chicken Purée

Chicken is an ideal first meat for your baby as it has a mild flavour and is easily digested. By introducing chicken at 6 months it is an excellent way to introduce texture into your baby's food as you move on from a runny vegetable purée to something more substantial. This purée is perfect to batch cook. Just make sure not to blend it, so that you can adapt it to suit your baby's age when you defrost.

Portions: 6 x 90ml/3oz

300ml low salt vegetable stock
1 onion, chopped
1 carrot, chopped
2 celery stalks, chopped
1 skinless chicken breast

1 Place a large saucepan over a medium heat and add the stock and vegetables. Bring to the boil.

2 Add the chicken breast and simmer for 15-20 minutes, until cooked through.

3 At this stage, if your baby is a little older and able for more texture, remove the chicken breast.

4 Transfer the vegetables and chicken to the blender and blend to the desired consistency.

5 If you have removed the chicken breast at step 3, flake on top of the vegetable purée.

6 Store portions in your weaning pots and freeze extras for future use.

 FREEZER FRIENDLY

PERFECT FOR TUMMIES | 6 MONTHS+

Chicken, Green Beans & Avocado

First Foods

This recipe makes having a roast dinner something that your baby can join in with too. Serve up the roast chicken and green beans with some potatoes for the rest of the family to enjoy.

Portions: 6 x 90ml/3oz

Olive oil
1 chicken breast on the bone
Handful of green beans
250ml low salt vegetable stock
1 avocado

> You can season your baby's chicken with a sprinkle of fine ground pepper but hold off on adding any salt.

1 Preheat the oven to 180°C degrees.

2 Gently rub both sides of the chicken with the olive oil. Place the chicken on a roasting tray and bake for 45 minutes.

3 Wash the green beans and cut the ends off. Place in an oven dish and drizzle with some olive oil. Cook in the oven for 30 minutes.

4 Remove the chicken from the bone. Place into a blender along with the vegetable stock and the green beans. Blend until you get the desired consistency.

5 At this stage its best to store portions in your weaning pots and freeze extras for future use.

6 To serve, mix 1 tbsp of mashed avocado with 3 tbsp of chicken purée.

 FREEZER FRIENDLY

PERFECT FOR TUMMIES | 6 MONTHS+

Breakfast

This is my girls' favourite meal of the day. My daughter loves a bowl of porridge and a smoothie so that she feels set up for the day ahead.

When it comes to breakfast, preparation is key so that you don't have to reach for shop bought alternatives. I have included some recipes for the time-pressed mum alongside recipes for those days when your have a little more time on your hands.

Banana & Berry Muffins

Breakfast

Muffins are a big hit in our house and the children really enjoy getting involved in making them. These are no exception! They make a healthy snack for lunch boxes or can be a fun alternative to the usual breakfast. I always make a big batch of muffins and freeze them so that I have them on hand as required. Then they just need heating up before serving.

Portions: 12 Muffins

125g plain flour
75g wholemeal flour
200g porridge oats
3 tsp baking powder
1 tsp cinnamon
1 tsp salt (omit for baby)
75g brown sugar (omit for baby)
3 tbsp sunflower oil
2 large eggs
250ml full fat milk
2 bananas, mashed
125g mixed berries

1 Preheat the oven to 200°C. Grease a muffin tin or line with paper cases.

2 Combine the flour, rolled oats, baking powder, cinnamon, salt and sugar.

3 In a separate bowl mix the sunflower oil, eggs and milk.

4 Make a well in the dry ingredients then pour in the wet and combine well.

5 Fold in your mashed banana and berries until everything is mixed evenly.

6 Divide the mixture into the muffin tin. Place in the oven for 20-25 minutes, until a knife inserted in the center of a muffin comes out clean.

 FREEZER FRIENDLY

PERFECT FOR TUMMIES | 6 MONTHS+

Porridge for Baby

Porridge is perfect for the whole family, including your weaning baby. Introduce porridge early to your baby so that they go on to eat it as a toddler. Porridge is filling and sustaining due to it's relatively rich protein levels. Alternative grains can be used such as millet, which is rich in B vitamins and makes a mild, sweet porridge. You can also use quinoa, which is often called a supergrain because it is rich in protein and key nutrients. Change it up each morning by adding yoghurt, fruit purées or chopped fruit.

Portions: 1 x Baby

15g porridge oats/ millet/ quinoa
150ml milk, water or a mixture

1   Add the oats and milk or water to a saucepan. Place over a medium heat and bring to the boil.

2   Once boiling, simmer for 4-5 minutes, stirring from time to time and making sure it doesn't stick to the bottom of the saucepan.

3   Remove from the heat, stir and leave to stand for 2-3 minutes before serving.

4   Serve with toppings of your choice such as berries, flaxseed or yoghurt.

PERFECT FOR TUMMIES   6 MONTHS+

Baby Muesli

Breakfast

This muesli makes a delicious and nutritious breakfast for your weaning baby. Soak in your choice of milk and store in the refrigerator to serve healthy breakfasts during the busy week. Muesli is so versatile and filling - I like to change it up each morning with different fruits like grated apple, banana, mixed berries or even fruit purée!

Portions: 5 x Baby

50g porridge oats
1 weetabix biscuit
1 tbsp desiccated coconut

For smaller babies soak overnight to give it a nice creamy texture. Add warm milk before serving.

1 Place all the ingredients in a food processor and blend to a fine powder.

2 Store blended muesli in airtight portion pots for up to 2 months.

3 To serve, soak the muesli in milk for at least 30 minutes, but preferably overnight in the refrigerator.

4 Top with grated apple or mixed berries for added texture.

PERFECT FOR TUMMIES | 6 MONTHS+

Coconut Muesli

―――――― ••• ――――――
Breakfast

This is a great breakfast, packed with a delicious combination of coconut, toasted nuts and seeds. It makes the perfect healthy meal for both baby and family, as soon as your baby is ready for some texture.

Portions: 16 x Baby

75g almonds (I use blanched)
50g sunflower seeds
50g desiccated coconut
4 tbsp wheat germ
300g porridge oats
1 tsp cinnamon

1 Place a pan over a low heat. Add the nuts and seeds and toast for 5 minutes, stirring constantly until golden brown. Remove from the heat and leave to cool for 5 minutes.

2 Transfer the cooled nuts and seeds to a food processor. Add the coconut and wheat germ.

3 Blend until a powdery consistency is reached and transfer to a large bowl. Mix in the oats and cinnamon.

4 To serve, add milk and allow it to soften for 5 minutes. Serve with fresh fruit or yoghurt. For a baby not able for texture, soak overnight.

Make up a batch for your baby and it will keep in your airtight portion pots for 2 months.

PERFECT FOR TUMMIES | 6 MONTHS+

Berry Overnight Oats

Breakfast

This recipe is a personal favourite when I know I have an early start to my day. It's quick and easy to put together the night before, and saves valuable time in the morning. Make it up in portion sizes for baby and family. Having a delicious breakfast couldn't be easier.

Portions: 1 x Adult

50g porridge oats
50g full fat natural yoghurt
50g frozen mixed berries

1 Layer each pot with yoghurt, then mixed berries and oats.

2 Repeat the layers until you have filled your pots.

3 Refrigerate overnight. Serve in the morning topped with fruits, nuts and seeds of your choice.

4 For your baby, mash the berries with the yoghurt and soft oats to serve.

Mix things up by using different fruits such as pear, banana and grated apple.

PERFECT FOR TUMMIES | 6 MONTHS+

Cinnamon French Toast

This is a tasty twist on the simple classic. Serve topped with berries and banana for natural sweetness and added nutrition. For your baby, simply slice the French toast up into fingers and serve with a mashed banana.

Portion: 1 x Baby Finger Food

1 tsp olive oil
A small knob of unsalted butter
1 egg
1 tbsp full fat milk
A dash of vanilla extract
1 slice of wholemeal bread

To serve:
Blueberries
½ banana, sliced
A sprinkle of cinnamon

1 Place a frying pan on a medium heat. Add the olive oil and butter.

2 Whisk the egg in a bowl. Add the milk and vanilla extract and combine.

3 Pick the bread up with a fork and dip back and front in the egg mixture.

4 Transfer to the preheated pan. Fry for a minute on either side until golden brown.

5 Serve topped with banana, blueberries and cinnamon.

PERFECT FOR TUMMIES | 6 MONTHS+

Boiled Egg & Avocado Toast

Breakfast

Boiled eggs are a quick and fuelling breakfast for your baby. When combined with avocado and wholemeal bread, they provide a perfectly nutritionally balanced start to the day. Cut it into slices to make a finger food for your weaning baby to self-feed. It can also be an easy midday feed for your baby.

Portions: 1 x Baby

1 egg
1 slice wholemeal bread
½ avocado, mashed

> Get your baby eating hard boiled eggs early to get them used to the taste and texture. They are the perfect high protein snack for a school-going child.

1 Place a small saucepan of water over a medium heat and bring to the boil.

2 Carefully add the egg to the water, using a slotted spoon if necessary.

3 Boil for 9 minutes to ensure the egg cooks through.

4 While cooking, pop the bread into the toaster.

5 Remove the egg from the water using a slotted spoon then allow to cool for 2 minutes before peeling the shell.

6 Slice the egg. Spread the avocado on the toast and top with the sliced egg.

PERFECT FOR TUMMIES	6 MONTHS+

Omelette Fingers

Omelette fingers are a fantastic finger food for your weaning baby. When your baby is able to manage some texture, you can add other ingredients, such as grated or chopped vegetables and herbs.

Portions: 1 x Baby

A small knob of unsalted butter
1 tsp rapeseed oil
1 egg
1-2 tsp Cheddar cheese, grated

1 Heat the butter and oil in a frying pan over a medium heat.

2 Beat the egg. Mix in the cheese.

3 Gently pour the egg into the pan, covering the pan with a thin layer.

4 Cook for a 2-3 minutes. Flip it over using a spatula, and cook for one more minute, or until completely set and slightly brown.

5 Allow to cool slightly. Slice into fingers to serve.

Omelettes keep well in a food flask and are perfect as a lunchbox filler for a school going child.

PERFECT FOR TUMMIES | 6 MONTHS+

Scrambled Eggs

These scrambled eggs are a quick and easy breakfast. Make sure they are cooked through if you are serving to your baby. For a bit of variety, add different vegetables like peppers as your baby gets accustomed to more texture.

Portions: 1 x Baby

1 tomato
1 egg
1 tbsp full fat milk
1 tsp unsalted butter
1 tbsp cheese
1 slice wholemeal bread, toasted

Use mild cheeses for baby. Cheddar is a great option.

1 Place a saucepan of water on a medium heat and bring to the boil.

2 Remove the pan from the heat. Add the tomato to blanch for 1 minute. Transfer to a clean paper towel and allow to cool.

3 In a bowl, whisk the egg and milk together.

4 Peel the cooled tomato and remove the seedy core. Chop the flesh and set aside.

5 Place a frying pan over medium heat and add the butter. Add the tomato and cook for 2 minutes.

6 Pour in the egg mixture. Cook for 2 minutes, breaking it up every few seconds using a wooden spoon or spatula. Sprinkle on the cheese and cook for a further 30 seconds.

7 Serve with strips of wholemeal toast as a finger food for your weaning baby.

PERFECT FOR TUMMIES	6 MONTHS+

Baby & Family Meals

My philosophy is simple: Cook for family first, adapt for baby.

We want everyone in the family eating well, so it's important to include your baby in your family meals. Prepare your recipes without salt and sugar, then blend or offer them as a finger food for your baby. Remember the only foods that can't be blended are white potato and pasta.

Chicken

Chicken is good source of protein, vitamins and minerals that your baby needs for growth and development. It's the best first meat to offer your baby because it blends well. Aim to introduce chicken at 6 months of age, so that your baby gets accustomed to the different texture. If offering as a finger food, cut the chicken in to thin slices or bite size pieces for your child to pick up.

Coconut Chicken Curry

Baby & Family Meals

I started making this recipe for my daughter, Ashleigh, at about 6 months of age. I think it is the reason she now likes all things spicy! I still prepare the same dish today and it's always a big hit.

Portions: 4 x Adults

1 tbsp olive oil
1 small red onion, finely chopped
1 garlic clove, minced
½ tbsp turmeric
1 tbsp curry powder
1 sweet potato, peeled and cubed
1 carrot, peeled and chopped
½ small head of cauliflower, chopped
4 tbsp red split lentils, soaked and washed
4 skinless chicken breasts, cubed
400ml coconut milk
60g frozen peas

1 Heat the oil in a large frying pan over a medium heat. Fry the onion for 3 minutes, until soft.

2 Mix in the garlic, turmeric and curry powder and cook for a further minute.

3 Add the vegetables, lentils and chicken. Stir well to coat everything evenly in the spices.

4 Pour in the coconut milk and bring the mixture to the boil. Cover and simmer for 20 minutes, stirring every 5 minutes. You'll know it's ready when the sweet potato is soft and the lentils have cooked through.

5 Stir in the peas and serve over your choice of rice. Remove your baby's portion and blend to the desired consistency.

 FREEZER FRIENDLY

PERFECT FOR TUMMIES | 6 MONTHS+

Chicken Fajitas

Baby & Family Meals

These chicken fajitas are so quick to make and full of flavour. Place the accompaniments in the center of your dinner table so that your children can get involved with making their own. This will make their mealtime even more enjoyable, and will encourage them to eat up. For baby, serve the chicken and peppers as a finger food.

Portions: 4 x Adults

4 skinless chicken breasts, sliced
1 red onion, sliced
1 red and yellow pepper, sliced
1 tbsp paprika
1 tbsp of coriander
A pinch of cumin
Juice of 1 lime
Drizzle of olive oil

Accompaniments:
Tortillas
Salsa
Sweetcorn
Crème fraiche or natural yoghurt
Grated cheese

1 Mix everything together in a bowl ensuring your chicken is evenly coated with the spices.

2 Heat your griddle pan over a high heat until very hot. Cook the coated chicken and vegetables for 6-8 minutes, or until the chicken is cooked through. Remove from the heat.

3 Put the chicken and vegetables into a bowl. Place on your dinner table along with heated tortillas, salsa, sweetcorn crème fraiche, and cheese.

4 For your baby, chop the chicken and vegetables into bite size pieces to self-feed.

 FREEZER FRIENDLY

PERFECT FOR TUMMIES 6 MONTHS+

Chicken & Pesto Courgetti

Baby & Family Meals

Courgetti is a fun and easy way to introduce courgettes to your child. This recipe is a healthy twist on a well-loved dish and is great for getting fussy eaters to enjoy their vegetables.

Portions: 4 x Adult

2 tbsp olive oil
4 skinless chicken breasts, sliced
2 courgettes, spiralised
4 tbsp basil pesto (*pg 163*)
160g spaghetti, cooked
Handful of cherry tomatoes
Parmesan to serve

If you don't have a spiraliser, use a peeler to ribbon the courgette.

1 Heat 1 tbsp of olive oil in a frying pan over a medium heat. Add the chicken and cook for about 5 minutes, or until cooked through.

2 Heat another frying pan with the rest of the olive oil. Cook the courgettes for 4-6 minutes.

3 Stir the pesto into the pan with the chicken then add the courgettes.

4 Add the spaghetti to your chicken and courgette. Add more pesto as desired. Plate up and top with grated Parmesan and cherry tomatoes.

5 For your baby, cut into bite size pieces to self-feed. This dish can also be blended without the spaghetti and offered as a purée.

 FREEZER FRIENDLY

PERFECT FOR TUMMIES | 6 MONTHS+

Chicken Parmigiana

Baby & Family Meals

Crispy breaded chicken covered in tomato sauce and topped with cheese. What's not to love? This recipe takes a little extra time but is definitely worth it. My children love bringing the leftovers in their food flasks to school for lunch the next day.

Portions: 4 x Adult

4 large, skinless chicken breasts
1 egg, beaten
75g breadcrumbs
75g Parmesan, grated
2 tbsp olive oil
2 cloves of garlic, minced
340g tomato passata
200g tin chopped tomatoes
1 tsp dried oregano
75g mozzarella, torn

1 Using a rolling pin, pound the chicken breasts between sheets of cling film until thin.

2 Mix the breadcrumbs with ⅔ of the Parmesan in a bowl. Dip the chicken into the egg, then coat with the breadcrumb mixture. Place them on a plate and refrigerate while you prepare the sauce.

3 Heat a saucepan over a medium heat. Sauté the garlic in 1 tbsp of olive oil for 1 minute. Add in the tomatoes, passata and oregano. Simmer for 5-10 minutes.

4 Add 1 tbsp of olive oil to a frying pan on a high heat. Fry the chicken for 5 minutes on each side until cooked through.

5 Pour the tomato sauce into a shallow oven-proof dish and place the chicken on top. Top with the mozzarella and the remaining Parmesan. Grill until the cheese has melted and the sauce is bubbling.

6 Serve with pasta or potato and your choice of vegetables. For your baby, blend to the desired consistency.

 FREEZER FRIENDLY

PERFECT FOR TUMMIES | 6 MONTHS+

Chicken Cacciatore

Baby & Family Meals

This Italian stew is perfect for batch cooking. I always freeze portions of it to have on hand for busier days. Although it pairs deliciously with rice, my children always insist on having it with mashed potatoes. For baby, exclude the chilli until they are used to stronger tastes.

Portions: 4 x Adult

1 tbsp olive oil
4 skinless chicken breasts, cubed
1 onion, finely chopped
2 red peppers, sliced
½ tbsp dried rosemary
½ tbsp dried thyme
2 cloves of garlic, minced
1 red chilli, de-seeded and sliced
175ml low salt chicken stock
2 x 400g tins chopped tomatoes
2 tbsp of tomato purée
Chopped parsley, to serve

1 Preheat the oven to 180°C.

2 Heat the oil in a deep, oven-proof frying pan that can fit the chicken in a single layer over a medium heat. Lightly brown the chicken for 5 minutes. Remove the chicken and set aside.

3 Add the onion, peppers, dried herbs, garlic and chilli to the frying pan. Cook for 10 minutes until they soften and the vegetables begin to brown.

4 Add in the stock, tomatoes and tomato purée. Stir well. Bring the mixture to the boil then return the chicken to the pan.

5 Cover and bake in your oven for 20 minutes. Remove the cover and bake for a further 15-20 minutes.

6 Once the chicken is fully cooked remove from the oven and sprinkle with parsley. Serve with rice, polenta or mashed potato. For your baby, blend to the desired consistency.

 FREEZER FRIENDLY

PERFECT FOR TUMMIES | 6 MONTHS+

Chicken & Chips

Baby & Family Meals

Every child loves chicken and chips! This is a healthier way to include it in your weekly meals. Shop bought chicken goujons are usually high in salt and preservatives and not suitable for your baby.

Portions: 4 x Adult

For the Chips:
4-5 floury potatoes (Maris Pipers)
2 tbsp olive oil
2 tsp smoked paprika

For the Fingers:
4 slices wholemeal bread
50g Parmesan cheese, grated
4 skinless chicken breasts, sliced
60g plain flour
2 eggs, whisked

1 Preheat the oven to 200°C. Peel the potatoes and chop into chips.

2 In a large bowl, mix the olive oil and paprika. Toss in the potatoes and mix until all of the chips are coated.

3 Use a food processor to blend the bread and Parmesan cheese into breadcrumbs.

4 Place the chicken, flour, eggs, and breadcrumb mixture into separate bowls. Place the bowls in a line.

5 Dip the chicken into the flour, followed by the egg, followed by the breadcrumbs. Place them on an roasting tray. (Get your children to take charge of this step for some fun in the kitchen).

6 Add the chips to the tray, making sure to spread them out (or use a second tray if needed). Bake for about 20 minutes. Turn the chicken and chips half way, to cook evenly.

7 Offer to your baby as a finger food.

 FREEZER FRIENDLY

PERFECT FOR TUMMIES 6 MONTHS+

Meat

Red meat is the best source of iron available. It is essential to promote healthy growth and prevent iron deficiency anaemia. When your baby is accepting food from a spoon, soft well-cooked meat can be puréed and blended with vegetables. You can also offer strips of cooked meat to your baby from 6 months. Aim to feed your child meat at least 3 times every week.

Chilli Con Carne

---•••---

Baby & Family Meals

Don't let the 'chilli' in the name put you off. You can increase or decrease the spices to suit your taste preference. For baby, add chilli powder as a first taste. Move onto extra chillies when you think your child is ready to accept food that is a little spicier. You will be surprised how much children love spices!

Portions: 6 x Adult

2 tbsp olive oil
2 onions, finely chopped
2 large carrots, finely chopped
2 celery sticks, finely chopped
1kg quality minced beef
4 garlic cloves, minced
1 red chilli, de-seeded and finely chopped
1 tsp mild chilli powder
2 heaped tsp paprika
2 red pepper, chopped
2 x 400g tins chopped tomatoes
2 x 400g tins kidney beans, drained
500ml low salt beef stock

1 Heat the olive oil in your largest pan. Add all your chopped vegetables and cook over a medium heat for 10 minutes, stirring every 30 seconds.

2 Add in the meat, garlic, chilli, paprika and peppers. Cook together for 5 minutes.

3 Add in the tomatoes, kidney beans and stock. Bring to a simmer.

4 Cook for 1 hour, with the lid on, stirring occasionally.

5 Serve straight away with rice, or allow to cool and freeze for future use.

6 For a baby not able for texture, blend the chilli con carne to the desired consistency. For more texture, mash and offer with some rice or potato.

 FREEZER FRIENDLY

PERFECT FOR TUMMIES | 6 MONTHS+

Lamb Curry

————— ••• —————

By cooking lamb for two hours, you get a lovely tender meat that your baby can enjoy. If you batch cook and freeze this recipe, your meat will be even more tender after you reheat it.

Portions: 4 x Adult

1 tbsp olive oil
1kg shoulder of lamb, cubed
1 large onion, finely chopped
3 cloves of garlic, minced
1 red chilli, de-seeded
and thinly sliced (optional)
1 tsp of grated ginger
1½ tbsp ground cumin
1 tsp ground coriander
1 tsp ground turmeric
400g tin chopped tomatoes
500ml low salt lamb or beef stock
1 bay leaf

1 Heat the oil in a large pan and brown the lamb. Remove from the pan and set aside.

2 In the same pan, cook the onions for 5-6 minutes. Add in the garlic and chilli and cook for a further 2 minutes. Add the ginger, cumin, coriander and turmeric.

3 Return the lamb to the pan along with the tomatoes, stock and bay leaf.

4 Bring the mixture to the boil. Reduce the heat and simmer uncovered for 1½-2 hours, until the meat is tender and the sauce has reduced.

5 For your baby, chop into bite size pieces to serve as a finger food. Or, for a baby not able for texture, blend to a purée, adding more stock to loosen the purée. Serve with mashed potato.

> If you prefer a thicker sauce, simply stir in some cornflour at the very end.

 FREEZER FRIENDLY

PERFECT FOR TUMMIES | 6 MONTHS+

Baby & Family Meals

This Greek dish is traditionally made with aubergines, however, in this recipe I use potatoes.

Portions: 4 x Adult

2 tbsp olive oil
1 onion, finely chopped
2 carrots, roughly chopped
2 cloves of garlic, minced
1 tbsp oregano
1 tbsp thyme
1½ tsp cinnamon
500g quality minced lamb
400g tin chopped tomatoes
2 tbsp tomato purée
235ml low salt vegetable stock
4 potatoes, peeled & thinly sliced
3 tbsp butter
3 tbsp plain flour
370ml full fat milk
380g Cheddar cheese, grated
1 egg, beaten

1 Preheat the oven to 200°C. Heat 1 tbsp of olive oil in a large pan. Cook the onions, carrots and garlic until they brown. Stir in the herbs and cinnamon.

2 Add the minced lamb and brown for 3-4 minutes. Stir in the chopped tomatoes, tomato purée and stock. Bring to the boil before reducing to a simmer for 30-40 minutes.

3 Meanwhile, heat 1 tbsp of olive oil in a frying pan. Brown the potatoes in batches, for 1-2 minutes on each side.

4 For the topping, melt the butter in a small saucepan and stir in the flour. Cook for 1 minute. Gradually whisk in the milk. Once thickened, remove from the heat and stir in the cheese. Allow to cool slightly before beating in the egg.

5 Line a casserole dish with half of the potatoes. Layer on the mince mixture and top with the remaining potatoes.

6 Pour the cheese sauce on top. Bake for 30-40 minutes, until it is fully cooked and the top is golden-brown.

7 For a baby not able for texture, blend the sauce and serve with mashed potato.

 FREEZER FRIENDLY

PERFECT FOR TUMMIES 6 MONTHS+

Shepherd's Pie

Baby & Family Meals

This is the ultimate Irish comfort food and was a favourite of mine growing up. In our house, it's called Nanny's Shepherd's Pie. It is always requested by my girls when they visit Nanny.

Portions: 4 x Adult

1 tbsp olive oil
1 onion, finely chopped
2 carrots, finely chopped
500g quality minced lamb
½ tbsp ground cinnamon
1 tbsp tomato purée
300ml low salt vegetable stock
Small handful of fresh thyme
2 potatoes, peeled and cubed
2 parsnips, peeled and cubed
2 tbsp butter
Small handful of Cheddar, grated
1-2 tbsp full fat milk
Large handful of frozen peas

1 Heat the oil in a saucepan over a medium heat. Soften the onion and carrots for a few minutes. Turn up the heat. Add the lamb and brown.

2 Mix in the cinnamon and tomato purée then fry for a few minutes. Add the stock and thyme. Bring to a simmer and cook for 30 minutes.

3 Meanwhile, preheat the oven to 180°C. Steam the potatoes and parsnips for 15-20 minutes, until tender. Mash them together. Mix in the butter, cheese and milk.

4 Stir the peas into the mince. Portion out into oven-proof dishes. Pipe on the mash and top with a few more peas.

5 For immediate use, bake the pies for 20-25 minutes, until the top starts to brown and the mince bubbles through at the edges. Leave to stand for 5 minutes before serving. To keep the pies for a later date, chill and freeze them.

6 For a baby not able for texture, blend the meat with the vegetables, and add the mashed potato before serving.

 FREEZER FRIENDLY

PERFECT FOR TUMMIES | 6 MONTHS+

Bolognese

— ••• —

Baby & Family Meals

This recipe is my favourite for batch cooking. It can be used in a lasagne or simply served over pasta. To save time, pulse your vegetables in a food processor rather than spending ages peeling and chopping.

Portions: 8 x Adult

1 tbsp olive oil
60g pancetta, chopped
2 onions, finely chopped
4 celery stalks, finely chopped
4 carrots, finely chopped
4 tbsp oregano
900g quality minced beef
4 cloves of garlic, minced
2 tbsp ground nutmeg
680g tomato passata
2 x 400g tins chopped tomatoes
4 tbsp tomato purée
200ml low salt beef stock
2 bay leaves

1 Heat olive oil in a pan. Fry the pancetta until it begins to crisp. Add the onions and cook until translucent. Transfer the onions and pancetta to a large pan.

2 Add the celery, carrots and oregano and sauté. Remove from the heat. Add to the large pan with the onions and pancetta.

3 Return the pan to the heat. Add the mince, garlic and the nutmeg. Cook until the mince is browned.

4 To the large pan add the browned mince, passata, chopped tomatoes, tomato purée, stock and bay leaves. Bring to the boil, mix through, reduce the heat and leave to simmer for 20-30 minutes.

5 To thicken the sauce, either bring back to the boil, simmer and reduce, or stir in 1 tbsp of cornflour. Remove the bay leaves before serving.

6 For a baby not able for texture, blend the mince and serve with small pasta shapes.

 FREEZER FRIENDLY

PERFECT FOR TUMMIES | 6 MONTHS+

Burgers with Hidden Veg

Baby & Family Meals

I love this recipe because it incorporates vegetables and spices. Although I am not a big fan of hiding vegetables, it is a great way of getting your children to eat vegetables that they might not otherwise accept.

Portions: 4 x Adult

1 courgette
1 red onion
Small handful of spinach
1 tsp smoked paprika
2 tbsp oregano
1 tsp garam masala
1 tsp ground cumin
1kg quality minced beef
1 egg
4 slices wholemeal bread, made into breadcrumbs
1 tbsp olive oil

1 Peel the courgette. Add to your food processor along with the onion and spinach.

2 Pulse the vegetables until smooth. Add in the spices and pulse again.

3 In a large bowl combine the beef, blended vegetables and egg.

4 Add in the breadcrumbs and form into burgers.

5 Heat the olive oil in a large frying pan over a medium heat. Cook the burgers in batches for 6-8 minutes on each side, until fully cooked.

6 Place on a wholemeal bun adding on your desired toppings such as cheese, onion, tomato, and spinach. Serve with a side of polenta chips *(pg 130)*.

7 For your baby, make small burgers the size of a meatball. Serve as a finger food.

 FREEZER FRIENDLY

PERFECT FOR TUMMIES | 6 MONTHS+

Meatballs

Baby & Family Meals

Another favourite in our household. My girls love helping roll out the meatballs. Involving children in the preparation of meals encourages them to eat foods they might otherwise avoid. Leftover meatballs make a great lunch for my children to bring to school in their food flasks!

Portions: 4 x Adult

1 onion, finely chopped
1 red pepper, finely chopped
½ tbsp oregano
½ tbsp ground cumin
½ tbsp paprika
1 tsp mild chilli powder
500g quality minced beef
1 egg
1 tbsp olive oil
1 portion of Homemade Tomato Sauce *(pg 137)*
300g spaghetti

1 Combine the onion, pepper, herbs and ground spices in a large bowl. Add in the mince and the egg. Mix thoroughly.

2 Use your hands to roll the mixture into meatballs. Set aside any meatballs for freezing.

3 Heat the olive oil in a large frying pan. Add the meatballs and cook for 8-10 minutes, until cooked through, turning regularly.

4 Once cooked, add the Homemade Tomato Sauce to the pan and let simmer for about 10 minutes. Prepare the spaghetti according to the packet instructions.

5 Offer the meatballs as a finger food. When preparing the vegetables in this recipe, make sure that they are finely chopped or blended in a food processor.

 FREEZER FRIENDLY

PERFECT FOR TUMMIES | 6 MONTHS+

Ashleigh's Tortilla Pizza

These are my daughter Ashleigh's favourite toppings. Using tortillas to create a double base stuffed with tomato sauce makes this an even more delicious and healthy alternative to shop bought or takeaway pizza.

Portions: 1 Pizza

2 tortilla wraps of choice
4 tbsp Homemade Tomato Sauce
(pg 137)
Cheddar cheese, grated
1 slice ham, torn
2 tbsp sweetcorn
Mozzarella, torn
2 tsp pesto *(pg 163)*

Get your children to choose their own toppings, encouraging them to choose at least one vegetable.

1 Preheat the oven to 180°C and line a baking tray with parchment paper.

2 Place the flour tortilla on the baking tray. Top with 2 table-spoons of tomato sauce and spread evenly.

3 Place another tortilla on top and press down. Top with 2 more tablespoons of tomato sauce.

4 Add a handful of grated cheese.

5 Add the ham and sweetcorn. Top the pizza with mozzarella and dot with teaspoons of pesto.

6 Bake for 10-12 minutes, until the cheese is melted and the tortillas are crispy.

7 Cut into fingers for your baby to self-feed from 6 months.

PERFECT FOR TUMMIES | 6 MONTHS+

Seafood

Introducing fresh fish to your baby at a young age is a great way to help them develop their palate. Start with white fish, such as cod, that has a mild taste. Progress by moving onto stronger flavoured fish, such as salmon, later in the weaning process. Always make sure to flake fish prior to serving or blending. This will prevent small bones from making their way into your baby's food.

Fish Curry

Baby & Family Meals

This curry combines creamy coconut milk with fresh fillets of fish to create a delicious family dinner with a kick. It's mild enough for your weaning baby - just make sure to remove any bones from the fish before blending or serving.

Portions: 4 x Adult

Salt and pepper to taste (omit salt for baby)
1 tsp turmeric
4 fillets skinless cod, cubed
3 tbsp olive oil
2 large onions, finely chopped
3 cloves of garlic, minced
Thumb of ginger, minced
1 tbsp curry powder
Handful of green beans
400ml coconut milk

1 Mix the salt, pepper and turmeric in a bowl. Add the cubed fish and gently coat. Take care not to break up the fish.

2 Heat 2 tbsp of olive oil in a frying pan. Fry the fish until it is cooked through and slightly crispy. Remove the fish and set aside.

3 Add 1 tbsp of oil in the pan. Fry the onion, garlic and ginger until soft and browned. Add the curry powder and stir to coat.

4 Stir in the green beans and coconut milk. Bring the curry to the boil before reducing to a low heat. Add the fish. Cover and simmer for 10 minutes.

5 Serve with boiled rice, or allow to cool and freeze.

6 Blend the curry for a baby not able for texture, or offer as a finger food.

 FREEZER FRIENDLY

PERFECT FOR TUMMIES | 6 MONTHS+

Mediterranean Baked Cod

Cod is the perfect first fish for baby due to it's mild flavour. This recipe is always a great hit at my weaning classes. It's really delicious and easy to prepare.

Portions: 4 x Adult

2 tbsp olive oil
4 tomatoes, quartered
2 red peppers, roughly chopped
2 tbsp balsamic vinegar
4 fillets skinless cod
Juice from half a lemon
Handful of basil leaves

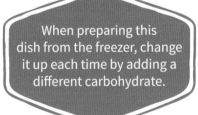

When preparing this dish from the freezer, change it up each time by adding a different carbohydrate.

1 Preheat the oven to 180°C. Grease a roasting tray with 1 tbsp of oil.

2 Add the tomatoes and peppers to the roasting tray. Drizzle the balsamic vinegar on top and then bake for 5 minutes.

3 Remove from the oven and place the cod fillets on top of the tomato and pepper mix. Top with the lemon juice and the rest of the oil.

4 Add the basil leaves and return to the oven. Bake everything for a further 15 minutes, until the fish is cooked through.

5 Transfer all the cooked vegetables to a food processor and blend to make the sauce.

6 Flake in your fish, ensuring all bones are removed. Serve with your choice of rice, quinoa or pasta.

7 For a baby not able for texture, you can blend the fish with the vegetables.

FREEZER FRIENDLY

PERFECT FOR TUMMIES | 6 MONTHS+

Pea & Prawn Risotto

This creamy risotto is one of our family favourites. It's perfect to whip up when you don't have any fresh ingredients in the house. It's ready in just 25 minutes!

Portions: 4 x Adult

1 litre low salt vegetable stock
50g unsalted butter
1 onion, finely chopped
1 tbsp oregano
250g Arborio rice
100g frozen peas
300g frozen prawns, thawed
Large handful of freshly grated Parmesan, plus extra to serve

To adapt for your baby, blend in a food processor, removing any shells from the prawns.

1 Place the stock in a large saucepan and bring to the boil. Reduce to a low simmer.

2 Heat half the butter in a large frying pan over a medium heat. Cook the onion and oregano for about 5 minutes, until soft.

3 Add the rice to the onion. Stir well, until all of the rice has been coated by the butter.

4 Add the stock, a ladle-full at a time, stirring frequently. Wait until all of the stock has been absorbed by the rice before adding another ladle-full.

5 After about 15 minutes, add in the peas. Stir well before continuing to add the stock.

6 Once all of the stock has been absorbed, add in the prawns.

7 Allow the prawns to cook in the mixture for a minute or two before removing the pan from the heat. Top with the remaining butter and Parmesan and cover. Let stand for at least 1 minute. Just before serving, give it a gentle stir.

PERFECT FOR TUMMIES	6 MONTHS+

Salmon Pasta with Courgetti

Baby & Family Meals

Omega-3 is vital for aiding brain health and development. This healthy, creamy salmon dish is a fantastic way of getting it into your little one's diet. Adding courgetti is a great way of boosting your family's vegetable intake.

Portions: 4 x Adult

350g tagliatelle
1 tbsp olive oil
3 courgettes
3 cloves of garlic, minced
2 sprigs of rosemary, chopped
450g of salmon, cubed
300g full fat cream cheese
Freshly ground black pepper
Juice of half a lemon

You cannot blend pasta so only offer this when your baby is ready for more textured meals.

1 Bring a large pan of water to the boil. Add the pasta and cook according to the instructions on the pack. Drain and leave to the side.

2 Meanwhile, spiralise your courgette or use a peeler to thinly slice length-ways.

3 Heat the oil in a large frying pan. Add the courgettes, garlic and rosemary. Cook until soft, but not golden.

4 Add the salmon cubes and the cream cheese and combine well. Cook for around another 5 minutes, until the salmon has cooked through.

5 Stir in the drained pasta. Season well with freshly ground pepper, and add lemon juice to taste.

4 For your baby, finely chop to serve.

 FREEZER FRIENDLY

PERFECT FOR TUMMIES | 9 MONTHS+

Mini Fish Pies

I love serving this up in mini ramekin dishes so the children can have their own portions. Fish pies are a great way to get your children to eat more fish.

Portions: 6 x Adult

625ml full fat milk
½ onion, finely chopped
6 peppercorns
1 bay leaf
700g skinless fish (e.g. haddock, salmon, hake)
100g unsalted butter
50g plain flour
25g frozen sweetcorn
25g frozen peas

For topping:
900g potatoes
25g Cheddar cheese, grated

1. Preheat the oven to 200°C.

2. Boil the potatoes until tender. Mash and set aside.

3. In a large saucepan bring the milk, onion, peppercorns and bay leaf to the boil, before reducing to a simmer. Add the fish and gently cook for 4-5 minutes. Remove the fish from the pan and set aside. Discard the bay leaf and peppercorn.

4. Melt the butter in an other saucepan over a medium heat. Stir in the flour to form a thick paste.

5. Stir the milk and onion mixture into the saucepan. Simmer until thickened.

6. Flake the fish into the sauce. Make sure to remove any bones. Add in the sweetcorn and peas.

7. Spoon the fish mixture into mini ramekin dishes. Top with mash potato then cheese. Bake for 15-20 minutes.

8. For a baby not able for texture, blend the fish mixture and serve with mashed potato.

 FREEZER FRIENDLY

PERFECT FOR TUMMIES | 6 MONTHS+

Vegetarian

We should all aim to have at least two vegetarian meals a week. They are much easier on our digestive system and are a great way of ensuring your child grows up loving their vegetables.

Sweet Potato & Chickpea Curry

Baby & Family Meals

Even Dad doesn't miss the meat when I serve up this dish. Adding chickpeas as a protein source makes it hearty and filling. If offering as a finger food for your baby, remove the chilli. If puréeing, you can include the chilli when blending if your baby likes a little bit of spice.

Portions: 4 x Adult

1 tbsp olive oil
2 red onions, finely chopped
1 tbsp mild curry powder
1 tbsp ground turmeric
½ red chilli, de-seeded and sliced
Handful of coriander leaves, finely chopped
400g tin chickpeas, drained
400g tin chopped tomatoes
3 sweet potatoes, cubed
400ml coconut milk
2 handfuls of spinach

1 Heat the olive oil in a large saucepan over a medium heat. Cook the onions for 10 minutes, until soft and golden. Stir in the curry powder and turmeric. Mix well.

2 Add in the chilli, coriander and chickpeas and cook for a further 5 minutes.

3 Add the tomatoes and sweet potato then bring to the boil. Reduce to a simmer, cover and cook for 15 minutes.

4 Remove the lid. Cook the curry for a further 10 minutes, stirring occasionally, until the sweet potato has cooked through and the sauce has thickened.

5 Stir in the coconut milk and bring the mixture to the boil. Turn off the heat stir in the spinach. Allow the curry to rest until the spinach is wilted. Serve as is, or alongside some rice, and enjoy!

6 If your baby is not able for texture, blend the curry to the desired consistency.

 FREEZER FRIENDLY

PERFECT FOR TUMMIES 6 MONTHS+

Pea and Parmesan Orzo

Baby & Family Meals

This orzo recipe is a simple and delicious family meal that your children are bound to love. Make sure to cook extra, so that you can double it up as a lunchbox filler.

Portions: 5 x Adult

2 tbsp unsalted butter
2 tbsp olive oil
1 onion, finely chopped
3 cloves of garlic, minced
500g orzo pasta
500ml low salt vegetable stock
Salt and pepper to taste
(omit salt for baby)
250g frozen peas
100g Parmesan cheese, grated

Find orzo pasta in most supermarkets or check your local health food store.

1 Over a medium heat, melt the butter and olive oil in a large saucepan.

2 Add the onions and stir continuously for about 3-4 minutes, until softened.

3 Add the garlic and orzo pasta then continue stirring for 1-2 minutes.

4 Pour in the vegetable stock. Add salt and pepper to taste.

5 Cook uncovered, stirring occasionally, until all the liquid has been absorbed into the pasta.

6 Stir in the peas and Parmesan. Cook until the Parmesan is melted and peas are heated through.

7 When your weaning baby is ready to accept texture, orzo pasta is the perfect option.

❄ FREEZER FRIENDLY

PERFECT FOR TUMMIES | 6 MONTHS+

Lentil Ragu

Baby & Family Meals

If you are like me and bolognese makes a regular appearance in your house, this recipe is the perfect vegetarian alternative. Don't try to fool your children into thinking it's meat-based bolognese. Instead, be honest and tell them it's something new.

Portions: 10 x Adult

1 tbsp olive oil
2 onions, finely chopped
2 cloves of garlic, minced
3 large carrots, finely chopped
3 celery sticks, finely chopped
500g red split lentils, soaked and drained
2 potatoes, cubed
2 x 400g tins chopped tomatoes
2 tbsp tomato purée
2 bay leaves
1 tsp dried oregano
1 litre low salt vegetable stock

1 Heat the olive oil in a large saucepan over a medium heat. Add the onions, garlic, carrots and celery.

2 Cook until softened, but not browned.

3 Add the lentils, potatoes, tomatoes, tomato purée, herbs and vegetable stock.

4 Bring to the boil, cover and simmer for 40-45 minutes, or until the lentils and vegetables are very tender.

5 Remove the bay leaf and serve over warm pasta. Or, store for future use.

6 For your baby, blend the ragu. Offer as a purée or coat the purée on penne pasta and offer as a finger food.

> Red split lentils have a soft texture and are rich in nutrients.

 FREEZER FRIENDLY

PERFECT FOR TUMMIES 6 MONTHS+

Mini Minestrone Soup

Baby & Family Meals

This delicious minestrone soup is great for weaning babies and children during cold winter days. You can use any kind of small pasta shapes. I like to use stellette star pasta shapes commonly used in soups. Serve it up with some toast fingers.

Portions: 4 x Adult

1 tbsp olive oil
2 onions, finely chopped
2 red peppers, finely chopped
1 courgette, grated
2 carrots, peeled and grated
700ml low salt vegetable stock
200g tin chopped tomatoes
120g stellette star pasta

1 Heat the olive oil in a large saucepan over a low heat. Cook the onions and peppers for 6-7 minutes, until soft.

2 Add the courgette, carrots, stock and tomatoes.

3 Bring to the boil. Cover and simmer for 20 minutes.

4 At this point, if you feel your baby might not accept the lumps, you can blend the vegetables.

5 Add in pasta. Cook for a further 10 minutes, until the pasta is soft.

6 Serve the soup immediately or store for future use.

This recipe is perfect in your Mummy Cooks Food Flask when you are out and about.

 FREEZER FRIENDLY

PERFECT FOR TUMMIES | 6 MONTHS+

Courgetti with Tomato Sauce

Baby & Family Meals

This is a great way to serve courgette to your children. My girls love helping me prepare it using the sprialiser. For children, it is important to always include a carbohydrate so serve pasta or crusty bread with this dish.

Portions: 4 x Adult

4 large courgettes
4 tbsp olive oil
2 onions, finely chopped
2 cloves of garlic, minced
4 tbsp dried oregano
1 tbsp paprika
1 tbsp ground coriander
2 tsp mild chilli powder
680g tomato passata
Handful of fresh basil, chopped
Parmesan cheese, grated

1 Sprialise the courgettes or use a peeler to make ribbons, and set aside. For fussy eaters who might reject it, peel the green skin.

2 Heat 2 tbsp of olive oil in a saucepan. Fry the onions until translucent. Add the garlic and cook for 2-3 minutes further.

3 Add the dried herbs and spices to the pan, followed by the passata. Bring the mixture to the boil, before simmering for 15-20 minutes, uncovered.

4 Mix in the basil and leave the sauce to sit.

5 In a large frying pan, add the remainder of the olive oil and cook the courgettes for about 5 minutes, until it has cooked through but is not soggy. Add the tomato sauce, and pasta if using, and coat well. Top with Parmesan cheese.

6 If your baby is not able for texture, blend the vegetables and tomato sauce, before adding the pasta.

| PERFECT FOR TUMMIES | 6 MONTHS+ |

Butternut Squash Risotto

Risotto is a favourite of mine. This recipe is creamy, delicious, and perfect for a weaning baby who is able for some texture. Introduce this to your family and it will soon become a popular and handy mid-week addition!

Portions: 4 x Adult

1 butternut squash, halved and de-seeded
2 tbsp olive oil
2 knobs unsalted butter
1 onion, finely chopped
1 tbsp dried oregano
250g Arborio rice
1 litre low salt vegetable stock
100g Parmesan cheese, grated

1 Preheat the oven to 180°C.

2 Place the butternut squash, cut side up, on a roasting tray. Drizzle 1 tbsp of the olive oil and dot 1 knob of the butter over the squash. Roast for 40 minutes, or until the squash is tender. Remove the skin and blend to a purée.

3 Bring the stock to the boil in a large saucepan, then simmer.

4 Heat the remaining oil and butter in a large frying pan over a medium heat. Add the onions and oregano. Cook until soft.

5 Stir the rice into the onions. Continue frying gently until the rice is opaque, but not browned.

6 Add in the stock a ladle-full at a time. Wait until all the stock has been absorbed by the rice before adding another ladle. Stir continuously. This takes about 20 minutes.

7 Mix in the squash purée and cheese. For a baby not able for texture, blend the risotto before serving.

 FREEZER FRIENDLY

PERFECT FOR TUMMIES | 6 MONTHS+

Ratatouille

This delicious, hearty dish is a great way to include a variety of vegetables into your family meals. Batch cook to have this on hand in the freezer to serve it as a healthy accompaniment to any meal. If you're serving this as your main meal, include rice or pasta on the side.

Portions: 4-6 x Adult

2 tbsp olive oil
2 aubergines, cubed
3 courgettes, cubed
3 peppers, cubed
4 cloves of garlic, minced
2 red onions, finely chopped
3-4 sprigs of fresh thyme, chopped
Handful of basil, chopped
400g tin chopped tomatoes
1 tbsp balsamic vinegar
Salt and pepper (omit salt for baby)

1 Heat 1 tbsp of olive oil in a large saucepan over a medium heat. Add the aubergines, courgettes, and peppers. Cook for about 5 minutes, until golden brown. Remove from the pan and set aside.

2 Heat the remaining olive oil. Add the garlic, onions, and chopped thyme. Cook for 10-15 minutes, until softened and golden.

3 Return the vegetables to the pan, then stir in the basil and tomatoes. Add the balsamic vinegar and a pinch of salt and pepper.

4 Simmer over a low heat for 30-35 minutes, stirring from time to time.

5 For a baby not able for texture, blend the ratatouille to the desired consistency. To serve as a finger food, offer as it is and let your baby self-feed.

 FREEZER FRIENDLY

PERFECT FOR TUMMIES | 6 MONTHS+

Polenta Chips

These chips are a great alternative to potato chips. Make them nice and crispy for your older children and they will love them. For your baby, they have a great texture to offer as a finger food.

Portions: 4 x Adult

1 litre low salt vegetable stock
350g polenta
25g Parmesan cheese, grated
Olive oil

> Use a cold surface, like stone, or place your tray in the freezer before setting the polenta.

1 Preheat the oven to 220°C. In a large saucepan, bring the vegetable stock to the boil.

2 Lower the heat and whisk in the polenta all at once. Keep whisking over a medium heat until it starts to thicken.

3 Remove from the heat and stir in the Parmesan cheese. Mix until the mixture has fully combined and has completely thickened.

4 Pour the mixture onto a chilled tray and allow to cool.

5 When the polenta has fully set, cut into chips.

6 Drizzle olive oil over a baking tray. Place the chips on the tray. Bake in the oven for 15-20 minutes, until golden and crispy. Turn half way through.

7 Serve and enjoy alongside our Burgers with Hidden Veg *(pg 100)* or Falafels *(pg 144)*.

8 Offer to your baby as a finger food.

| PERFECT FOR TUMMIES | 6 MONTHS+ |

Spicy Pumpkin Soup

Baby & Family Meals

This soup is a delicious way of turning any leftover pumpkin from Halloween into a healthy, nutritious dish. It's the perfect warming recipe to enjoy on a cold winters day. Leave out the chilli or add more to suit your family.

Portions: 4 x Adult

1 tbsp olive oil
2 onions, chopped
2 cloves of garlic, minced
1 red chilli, finely chopped
2 tbsp ground cumin
550g pumpkin, peeled and cubed
700ml low salt vegetable stock
400ml coconut milk
Handful of fresh coriander

1 Heat the olive oil in a large saucepan over a medium heat. Cook the onions for 3-5 minutes, until translucent.

2 Add the garlic, chilli and cumin then cook for a further 2 minutes.

3 Stir in the pumpkin and cook for a further 2-3 minutes.

4 Add the stock and bring the mixture to the boil. Reduce the heat and simmer with the lid on for 20-25 minutes.

5 Once the pumpkin is nice and tender, blend everything together before stirring in the coconut milk.

6 Garnish with some coriander to serve.

7 If you are making this for a baby, reduce the stock to 500ml and serve as a purée.

Butternut squash can be used instead of pumpkin.

❄ FREEZER FRIENDLY

PERFECT FOR TUMMIES | 6 MONTHS+

133

Creamy Mushroom Sauce

Baby & Family Meals

Mushrooms are a flavourful food and come in a great variety of textures and tastes. My girls are skeptical about mushrooms, but they will accept them in this creamy sauce. This sauce's consistency is great for your weaning baby and pairs well with pasta or chicken.

Portions: 4 x Adult

1 tbsp olive oil
3 spring onions, finely chopped
300g mushrooms, sliced
1 tsp fresh parsley, finely chopped
Freshly ground black pepper
100ml low salt vegetable stock
430g full fat cream cheese

1 Heat the olive oil in a large saucepan over a medium heat. Add the spring onions and cook until soft.

2 Add the mushrooms and cook until golden.

3 Add the parsley and black pepper. Pour in the stock. Stir well.

4 Cook over a low heat until the mushrooms are soft. Stir in the cream cheese.

5 Serve with your choice of pasta or potatoes.

6 If your baby is not able for texture, blend the mushroom sauce or chop into bite size pieces.

Introduce mushrooms early so your baby will learn to love the texture.

FREEZER FRIENDLY

PERFECT FOR TUMMIES | 6 MONTHS+

Homemade Tomato Sauce

Baby & Family Meals

I love making my own tomato sauce because there is no added salt or sugar. This makes it perfect for a weaning baby. Make sure to batch cook and freeze portions to have on hand for busier days. It's so versatile and pairs perfectly with meatballs, pasta, pizzas and more.

Portions: 4 x Adult

4 tbsp olive oil
4 cloves of garlic, minced
1 tbsp tomato purée
2 x 400g tins chopped tomatoes
Handful of basil, chopped

My girls and I love this sauce chunky, so we don't blend it for long.

1 Heat the olive oil in a large saucepan over a medium-low heat. Add in the garlic and cook for 3-4 minutes.

2 Stir in the tomato purée and cook for a further 2 minutes. Add in the chopped tomatoes.

3 Bring the mixture to the boil. Reduce the heat and simmer for 15-20 minutes, until the sauce has thickened.

4 Stir in the basil and simmer for a further 3-4 minutes.

5 Place the sauce in a blender or food processor and blend to your desired consistency.

6 Serve with pasta or portion and freeze for future use.

 FREEZER FRIENDLY

PERFECT FOR TUMMIES | 6 MONTHS+

Roasted Veg Pasta Sauce

Baby & Family Meals

Roasting vegetables brings out their sweetness, which makes this sauce one that even the most reluctant vegetable eaters will love. It's perfect served with pasta, meatballs or with garlic bread. Your children will definitely want this in their lunchbox, so make sure to cook a big batch.

Portions: 4 x Adult

1 onion, chopped
1 aubergine, chopped
1 courgette, chopped
1 red pepper, chopped
1 yellow pepper, chopped
1 green pepper, chopped
3 garlic cloves
1 tbsp olive oil
400g tin whole tomatoes
410ml low salt vegetable stock
3 tbsp balsamic vinegar

1 Preheat the oven to 200°C.

2 Place your chopped vegetables and garlic on a roasting tray and drizzle with olive oil.

3 Roast for about 20-25 minutes, until vegetables are soft and slightly brown on the edges. Turn them over half way through cooking.

4 Transfer your roasted vegetables to a large saucepan and add the tomatoes and vegetable stock.

5 Bring to the boil. Cover the pan and simmer for 20 minutes. Let cool. Transfer to the blender.

6 Add the balsamic vinegar to the blender and blend. Serve with pasta of your choice.

7 For your weaning baby, use on small pasta shapes or fusilli pasta and serve as a finger food.

 FREEZER FRIENDLY

PERFECT FOR TUMMIES | 6 MONTHS+

Finger Foods & Sauces

In this section I have included recipe ideas for delicious finger foods that the whole family will enjoy, as well as my favourite sauces to dip them in.

After initially introducing purées to your baby, you can offer meals as a finger food by simply not blending. Aim to serve one meal per day as a finger food to encourage independent feeding. This should lead to a happier and more accepting baby.

Roasted Sweet Potato Fingers

Finger Foods & Sauces

Introducing finger foods as early as 6 months gives your baby plenty of time to practice the pincer grasp – picking up objects with their thumb and forefinger. This recipe is an ideal first finger food for your weaning baby and is very easy to prepare.

Portions: 8 x Finger Food

1 sweet potato
Ground cinnamon

Try out different spices like nutmeg or curry powder.

1   Preheat the oven to 180°C.

2   Wash and pierce the sweet potato with a knife a few times.

3   On a roasting tray, bake the sweet potato in its skin, until tender. It usually takes about 40 minutes, depending on the size.

4   Leave to cool. Carefully remove the skin.

5   Cut into finger size pieces, then sprinkle with cinnamon.

6   For a baby starting off with finger food, place a finger size piece in the palm of their hand. For a baby who has grasped the pincer grasp, chop into bite size pieces and allow your child to pick up and self-feed.

 FREEZER FRIENDLY

PERFECT FOR TUMMIES | 6 MONTHS+

Baked Falafels

Usually falafels are fried, but this healthier version is baked. They team really well with one of my hummus recipes on *page 164* as a finger food meal for your baby. You could also serve them in a wrap for a school going child.

Portions: 10 x Falafels

2 x 400g tins chickpeas, drained
1 small onion
2 cloves of garlic
2 large handfuls of parsley
2 large handfuls of coriander
2 tsp ground cumin
3 tbsp olive oil

1 Preheat the oven to 200°C and line a baking tray with parchment paper.

2 Add all of the ingredients to a food processor and blend until combined, but not completely smooth.

3 Form the mixture into little logs. Adapt the size to suit your baby's hand.

4 Place the falafels on the prepared baking tray.

5 Bake for about 20 minutes, rolling over each falafel halfway through.

6 Serve immediately or store in portion pots for future use.

Use olive oil on your hands when shaping the mixture to help it bind.

 FREEZER FRIENDLY

PERFECT FOR TUMMIES | 6 MONTHS+

Broccoli & Cheese Muffins

Finger Foods & Sauces

Muffins are an ideal meal for your baby. They're also great as a vegetable filled snack in your child's lunchbox. Make a few batches and store them in your freezer so you always have a healthy savoury snack on hand.

Portions: 12 x Muffins

6 broccoli florets
230g self raising flour
120g Cheddar cheese, grated
6 cherry tomatoes, chopped
180ml full fat milk
3 tbsp olive oil
1 egg, beaten

1 Preheat the oven to 180°C. Grease a muffin tin.

2 Steam or boil the broccoli florets until tender. Leave to cool, then chop.

3 In a bowl, mix together the flour, cheese and broccoli.

4 Add in the tomatoes, milk, oil and egg then mix together thoroughly.

5 Spoon the batter into the muffin tin. Bake for 25-35 minutes until golden.

6 Offer a muffin to your weaning baby as a finger food along with some soup or hummus to dip.

FREEZER FRIENDLY

PERFECT FOR TUMMIES | 6 MONTHS+

Cauliflower Cheese Bites

Finger Foods & Sauces

This is one of my most popular recipes. Cauliflower is a favourite of mine, but it did take a while to get my children to share the love. Adding cheese definitely makes it easier. The shape of these bites make them the perfect finger food for your weaning baby.

Portions: 9 x Bites

1 small head of cauliflower
125g Cheddar cheese, grated
1 egg
1 tbsp oregano

You can also use a mix of 90g Cheddar and 30g Parmesan and switch the oregano for 1 tsp nutmeg for a different flavour combination.

1 Preheat the oven to 200°C and line a baking tray with parchment paper.

2 Separate the cauliflower into florets and boil or steam for 10 minutes, until tender. Run the cauliflower under cold water and drain completely.

3 Place in a food processor and gently pulse until it is broken up and looks like rice.

4 In a large bowl, combine the cauliflower, cheese, oregano and egg.

5 Using your hands, shape the cauliflower into patties.

6 Place the patties on the tray and bake for 10 minutes. Flip over and bake for a further 10 minutes.

7 Once the bites are golden brown, remove from the oven and allow to cool slightly before serving.

 FREEZER FRIENDLY

PERFECT FOR TUMMIES 6 MONTHS+

Sweet Potato Tots

Finger Foods & Sauces

The combination of sweet potato and cheese makes this a delicious finger food for your baby and the rest of the family. They are great served with tomato sauce for dipping.

Portions: 24 x Tots

3-4 sweet potatoes, cubed
125g Parmesan cheese, grated, plus more for rolling

Freeze and then heat in the oven for a super quick snack for your baby.

1 Preheat the oven to 200°C and line a baking tray with parchment paper.

2 Steam the sweet potato until you can pierce it with a fork, but it is still too tough to eat.

3 Put the sweet potatoes and Parmesan cheese into a food processor. Pulse a few times to achieve a chunky mashed texture.

4 Add the mixture into a large bowl. Form into small balls with your hands and then roll each tot in more Parmesan cheese to lightly coat.

5 Place the tots on the baking tray. Bake in the oven for 15 minutes, turning them once half way through, until golden.

6 Serve as a finger food for your baby to self-feed.

 FREEZER FRIENDLY

PERFECT FOR TUMMIES | 6 MONTHS+

Broccoli Tots

These healthy broccoli tots are a great way to get your children to eat more green vegetables. Broccoli and cheese work really well together, so even the fussiest of eaters should enjoy.

Portions: 20 x Tots

1 head of broccoli
1 egg
125g Cheddar cheese, grated
1 tsp garlic powder

1 Preheat the oven to 200°C and line a baking tray with parchment paper.

2 Separate the broccoli into florets then steam or boil until tender.

3 Once the broccoli is cooked, place it in a food processor and pulse until it has a rice-like consistency.

4 Add the broccoli to a large bowl, stir in the egg, cheese and garlic powder.

5 Once the mixture is combined, shape into tots.

6 Place the tots on the baking tray. Bake in the oven for 15-20 minutes until golden. Turn them once halfway through. Let the tots cool slightly before serving.

FREEZER FRIENDLY

PERFECT FOR TUMMIES | 6 MONTHS+

Mac & Cheese Muffins

Finger Foods & Sauces

My children actually came up with this recipe! They love both macoroni and cheese and muffins, so this was the perfect combination. I added the cauliflower to make sure we get our vegetable intake.

Portions: 6 x Muffins

1 small head of cauliflower, finely chopped
160g dried macaroni
3 tbsp unsalted butter
3 tbsp flour
350ml full fat milk
350g Cheddar cheese, grated

1 Preheat the oven to 190°C. Grease a muffin tin.

2 Bring a large saucepan of water to the boil. Add the dried macaroni and cauliflower and cook for 6-8 minutes. Strain off and allow to cool.

3 Meanwhile, in a small saucepan melt the butter. Stir in the flour until it forms a paste. Gradually whisk in the milk, until smooth without lumps.

4 Bring the mixture to the boil. Remove from the heat and stir in ⅔ of the cheese.

5 Stir the sauce into the macaroni and cauliflower mix.

6 Spoon the mix in the muffin tin and scatter the remaining cheese over the top.

7 Bake for 20 minutes. Remove from the oven and allow to cool before removing from the tin.

8 Offer to your baby as a finger food when they are able to manage soft lumps.

 FREEZER FRIENDLY

PERFECT FOR TUMMIES | 9 MONTHS+

Vegetable Muffins

Finger Foods & Sauces

If you are looking to get more vegetables into your children's diets, these muffins are the perfect choice. They make a great finger food for baby and a tasty lunchbox filler for a school going child. They are also a nice pick-me-up for busy parents who are always on the go.

Portions: 12 x Muffins

230g self raising flour
120g Cheddar cheese, grated
3 tbsp olive oil
180ml full fat milk
1 egg, beaten
1 courgette, grated
1 carrot, grated
Small handful of spinach, finely chopped
4 tbsp sweetcorn
1 small onion, finely chopped

1 Preheat the oven to 200°C. Grease a muffin tin.

2 In a bowl, mix together the flour and cheese.

3 In a seperate bowl, combine the oil, milk and egg.

4 Add the vegetables to the bowl with the flour and cheese. Stir in the wet ingredients and mix thoroughly until well combined.

5 Divide evenly into your muffin tin. Bake for 25-30 minutes, until golden brown and fully cooked through.

6 Allow to cool before serving.

 FREEZER FRIENDLY

PERFECT FOR TUMMIES | 6 MONTHS+

Sausage Rolls 4 Ways

Finger Foods & Sauces

Sausage rolls are a big hit with children, but most shop bought rolls are processed and can contain a high quantity of salt. Homemade is best when feeding your children. Here we have four different versions. Get the older children involved in assembling them!

Portions: 8 x Rolls

1 pack puff pastry
Chosen filling
1 egg, beaten

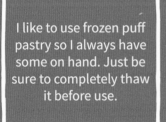

I like to use frozen puff pastry so I always have some on hand. Just be sure to completely thaw it before use.

1 Preheat the oven to 180°C and line a baking tray with parchment paper. Remove the pastry from the freezer and set on the counter top to soften.

2 Prepare your chosen filling from the recipes on the next pages.

3 Roll out the pastry and cut it in half length ways to form two long strips.

4 Spoon the filling evenly down the middle of each pastry strip.

5 Fold the pastry over the filling and seal with your hands or a fork. Brush with egg and cut the roll into 8 pieces.

6 Bake for 20-30 minutes until crispy, golden and thoroughly cooked. Allow to cool before serving.

7 Offer to your baby as a finger food to self-feed. You can place it in their hand, or chop into bite size pieces.

FREEZER FRIENDLY

PERFECT FOR TUMMIES | 9 MONTHS+

Chickpea Veggie Rolls

400g tin chickpeas, drained
1 courgette, grated
1 carrot, grated
1 clove of garlic, minced
½ onion, roughly chopped
1 tbsp oregano

1   Add the chickpeas, grated vegetables, garlic, onion and oregano to a food processor. Blend for 30-40 seconds.

2   Transfer to a large bowl and cover. Place in the fridge for 15 minutes to set.

Feta, Spinach & Tomato Rolls

1 tbsp olive oil
1 onion, finely chopped
4 medium tomatoes, cubed
60g spinach, chopped
Small handful of basil
200g feta cheese

1   Heat the olive oil in a frying pan over a medium heat. Add the onions and sauté for 2 minutes.

2   Add the tomatoes and cook for 3 minutes.

3   Once softened, add the spinach and basil then cook for a further 3 minutes.

4   Once cooked, drain the excess liquid and crumble feta cheese into the mixture.

Pork Sausage Rolls

300g quality minced pork
1 onion, finely chopped
2 cloves of garlic, minced
1 carrot, grated
1 courgette, grated
3 tbsp flour or breadcrumbs
2 tsp coriander

1 Place the pork, onion, garlic and grated vegetables in a food processor. Blend for 20-30 seconds.

2 Add the coriander and flour or breadcrumbs to the pork mix and blend until combined.

Turkey Apple Rolls

2 small apples
300g quality minced turkey
1 onion, finely chopped
1 carrot, peeled and grated
2 tbsp flour or breadcrumbs
1 tsp dried thyme

1 Peel, core and chop the apples. Add to a saucepan with 100ml of water. Bring to the boil, reduce heat and simmer for 5 minutes. Remove from the heat.

2 Blend the apples and cooking water in a food processor to form a smooth, thick purée. Add more water as required.

3 Add the other ingredients to the food processor. Blend for 20 seconds, until everything is combined.

Sweetcorn Muffins

Finger Foods & Sauces

The sweetness of the sweetcorn makes these savory muffins taste delicious. To make this recipe suitable for a baby from 6 months, substitute the honey for maple syrup and offer only on occasion.

Makes: 12 x Muffins

165g tin sweetcorn, drained
6 spring onions, roughly chopped
8 tbsp Greek yoghurt
60g unsalted butter, melted and cooled
2 tbsp honey
2 eggs
165g plain flour
1 tsp bicarbonate of soda
1 tsp baking powder
½ tsp salt (omit for baby)
¼ tsp paprika
100g Cheddar cheese, grated

1 Preheat the oven to 180°C. Line your muffin tin with paper cases.

2 Pulse the sweetcorn and spring onions in a food processor until blended.

3 Add in the yoghurt, butter, honey and eggs and blend until combined.

4 Mix the flour, bicarbonate of soda, baking powder, salt and paprika in a large bowl. Mix in the cheese.

5 Add the sweetcorn mixture to the dry ingredients. Combine well.

6 Spoon into muffin cases. Bake for 18 minutes, or until risen and firm to touch.

7 Allow to cool in the tin for a few minutes. Transfer to a wire rack and cool completely before serving.

 FREEZER FRIENDLY

PERFECT FOR TUMMIES | 12 MONTHS+

Pesto 3 Ways

Finger Foods & Sauces

Forget about shop bought pesto. Homemade versions taste much better and are salt free. Have these on hand to use as a sandwich spread, a dip for your baby's finger food or to stir through some pasta for an easy meal.

Each yields about 250g of pesto. To toast the pine nuts, toss them in a frying pan over a high heat for a about a minute. Place all the ingredients in a blender and blend until combined.

Basil Pesto

A classic the whole family will love

50g pine nuts, toasted
Large bunch of basil leaves
½ garlic clove
35g Parmesan, grated
100ml extra virgin olive oil
Squeeze of lemon juice
Ground black pepper

Pistachio Pesto

Perfect if you are feeling a bit adventurous

50g pistachios
50g mint
1 clove of garlic
35g Parmesan, grated
100ml extra virgin olive oil
Squeeze of lemon juice

Kale Pesto

Pesto with an even healthier and nutritious kick

50g pine nuts, toasted
3 handfuls of kale leaves
½ clove of garlic
35g Parmesan, grated
100ml extra virgin olive oil
Squeeze of lemon juice
Ground black pepper

 FREEZER FRIENDLY

PERFECT FOR TUMMIES | 6 MONTHS+

Hummus 3 Ways

Finger Foods & Sauces

Hummus is such a versatile dip, full of nutrients and flavour. Spread some on your children's sandwiches for lunch, or serve as a dip with finger foods for your weaning baby. My three versions are sure to be a hit with the entire family.

Each yields 400g of hummus. Just blend all the ingredients together until smooth. Freeze any extra in portion pots for future use.

Classic
Simple and delicious

400g tin chickpeas, drained
½ clove garlic
4 tbsp tahini
Juice of ½ lemon
4 tbsp Greek yoghurt (add more
for a creamier texture)

Coriander & Lime
Refreshing and tangy

400g tin chickpeas, drained
Small handful of coriander
2 tsp ground cumin
Juice of 1 lime
4 tbsp tahini

Red Pepper
With a kick

3 red peppers, roasted & peeled
400g tin chickpeas, drained
1 clove of garlic
¼ red chilli, de-seeded
1 small onion, sautéed
½ tsp ground cumin
1 tsp ground coriander
Squeeze of lemon juice
1 tbsp extra virgin olive oil

 FREEZER FRIENDLY

 **PERFECT FOR TUMMIES** | 6 MONTHS+

Pancakes

I have a Saturday ritual in our house of cooking pancakes with the girls. I use a very simple recipe and always make small round shapes so there is not much difficulty in flipping them over. I have included both savoury and sweet varieties in the following recipes.

Pumpkin Pancakes

Pancakes

If you're looking for a savoury take on the classic pancake, give these a try! The spiciness of the ginger mixed with cinnamon is the perfect complement to pumpkin. Even the pickiest eaters will be asking for more.

Portions: 12 x Pancakes

65g wholemeal flour
95g plain flour
2 tsp baking powder
1 tsp cinnamon
1 tsp ground ginger
240ml full fat milk
1 tbsp oil, plus more for the pan
1 egg
60g pumpkin, baked and puréed

1 Mix all the dry ingredients in a bowl and make a well.

2 In another bowl, whisk the milk, oil and egg together. Add the wet ingredients to the dry and mix well.

3 Add the puréed pumpkin and stir.

4 Lightly grease a large frying pan with oil and place over a medium heat.

5 For each pancake, pour a ladle of the batter on the pan and cook for about 2 minutes. When you see bubbles rising to the top, use a spatula to flip over and cook on the other side for a further 2 minutes.

6 Serve with your favourite toppings.

 FREEZER FRIENDLY

PERFECT FOR TUMMIES | 6 MONTHS+

Easy Plain Pancakes

Pancakes

This very simple, baby-friendly recipe is a wonderful way to teach your children to cook. They're brilliant for mixing up with different toppings or fillings. We love to eat ours topped with a mixture of berries, yoghurt and syrup.

Portions: 12 x Small Pancakes

½ cup wholemeal flour
½ cup self raising flour
1 cup full fat milk
1 egg
Knob of unsalted butter

1 Whisk the flour, milk and eggs together until smooth.

2 In a large frying pan, melt the butter over a medium heat.

3 Add your pancake mixture, one spoonful at a time. Cook until you see bubbles rising to the top. Flip over and cook on the other side for two minutes further.

4 Refrigerate leftover pancake mixture for up to two days, or cook extra and add to your child's food flask.

> Using cup measurements to make pancakes is quicker and a lot easier. Just make sure you're using the same cup size throughout!

 FREEZER FRIENDLY

PERFECT FOR TUMMIES | 6 MONTHS+

Potato & Parsnip Pancakes

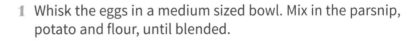

Pancakes

Surprisingly tasty, this is a great version of a savory pancake. Serve with tomato or pesto sauce for your child's lunch.

Portions: 9 x Small Pancakes

3 eggs
85g parsnip, grated
140g potato, grated
40g wholemeal flour
Knob of unsalted butter

1 Whisk the eggs in a medium sized bowl. Mix in the parsnip, potato and flour, until blended.

2 Melt the butter in a large frying pan over a medium heat. Add your pancake mixture, one tablespoon at a time.

3 Fry for 3 minutes on each side until lightly browned and cooked through.

Swap the usual rice and potatoes, and offer these pancakes as part of your child's main meal.

FREEZER FRIENDLY

PERFECT FOR TUMMIES | 6 MONTHS+

Banana Pancakes

Pancakes

For the most part, my children will eat everything, or at least try everything I offer them. I do however, have a problem with getting them to eat a banana. I think it may have something to do with how many bananas they ate as a baby. It was such a convenient food that I ended up overutilising it. This recipe has been a great way to get bananas, which are rich in fibre and potassium, back into their diet.

Portions: 8 x Small Pancakes

1 large banana
2 eggs, whisked
Knob of unsalted butter

1 Mash the banana as much as you can and then add in the eggs.

2 Melt butter on a frying pan over a medium heat.

3 Add spoonfuls of the mixture to the pan and then cook for 2 minutes, or until the bottom is set. Flip the pancake over and cook for a further minute.

It's best not to use a blender for this recipe as it will result in pancakes that are difficult to flip over.

 FREEZER FRIENDLY

PERFECT FOR TUMMIES 6 MONTHS+

Healthy Snacks & Treats

Snacks are important to keep your child fuelled and help maintain blood sugar levels, enabling them to feel energised and alert.

When your child reaches 9 months of age you will start to introduce 1 to 2 snacks per day at mid-morning and mid-afternoon. They are the perfect way to get more fruit and vegetables into your child's diet. This section contains a mixture of pantry snacks and cooked snacks, which are both healthy and nutritious. Most of these are easy recipes that the children can help out with.

10 Easy Pantry Snacks

Healthy Snacks & Treats

Every parent needs a range of simple snacks that can be assembled from standard pantry staples. The following is a list of pantry snacks that are quick to make. They are the perfect solution for staying healthy during busy days.

Aim to leave at least a 2 hour gap between your child's snack and their main meal.

1. Natural yoghurt topped with chopped fruit (or grated fruit for baby).

2. Apple slices and nut butter with toppings such as dried apricot, desiccated coconut or fruit.

3. Grated, sliced or cubed cheese with crackers.

4. Nut or seed butters spread on crackers, toast or rice cakes.

5. Mashed avocado on crackers, pitta or toast.

6. Sliced fresh fruit, e.g. strawberries.

7. Vegetable sticks, e.g. carrots, peppers or cucumber with hummus dip.

8. Halved cherry tomatoes and mozzarella balls.

9. Rice cakes (salt-free) with cheese spread.

10. Clementines and pitted cherries.

PERFECT FOR TUMMIES | 9 MONTHS+

Coconut Bites

These coconut bites are a real treat and so simple. Your children will love helping you make them. As this recipe contains free sugar, only offer to your weaning baby on occasion from 9 months.

Portions: 12 x Bites

200g desiccated coconut
130ml coconut oil, melted
3 tbsp maple syrup

Topping:
Dark chocolate, melted

1 Add the ingredients to your food processor and blend for a few minutes. Aim for a creamy texture rather than simply mixing.

2 Roll the mixture into balls and place on a baking tray lined with parchment paper.

3 Place the baking tray into the freezer for about half an hour to set.

4 Remove from the freezer and drizzle melted dark chocolate on top. Return to the freezer for 5 minutes.

5 To serve, remove from the freezer. Allow the bites to come to room temperature before offering to your child.

FREEZER FRIENDLY

PERFECT FOR TUMMIES | 9 MONTHS+

Apple, Oat & Sultana Muffins

Healthy Snacks & Treats

These muffins are packed with healthy ingredients, and are not too sweet, which makes them perfect for breakfast or as a midday snack. They are best served warm so make a batch, freeze any extra muffins and heat through before serving.

Portions: 12 x Muffins

100g plain flour
100g wholemeal flour
50g porridge oats
3 tsp baking powder
1 tsp ground cinnamon
50g caster sugar
2 medium red apples, peeled and grated
1 egg
125ml natural full fat yoghurt
125ml full fat milk
50ml rapeseed oil
75g sultanas

1 Preheat the oven to 190°C. Grease a muffin tin.

2 Mix together the flours, oats, baking powder, cinnamon and sugar.

3 Stir in the grated apple, making sure it is evenly distributed.

4 Whisk the egg together with the yoghurt, milk and oil in a separate bowl. Add to the dry mixture, and then add your sultanas. At this stage, it is important to mix gently until everything is well combined.

5 Spoon the mixture into the muffin tin then bake for 25-30 minutes until risen and golden brown.

6 Transfer to a wire rack to cool. Serve immediately or freeze for future use.

 FREEZER FRIENDLY

PERFECT FOR TUMMIES | 12 MONTHS+

Roasted Chickpeas

I always make sure to have a tin of chickpeas on hand so that I can whip up this delicious snack quickly. My children love experimenting with the flavours, but this is my favourite mix. Try it out with your weaning baby when they can manage some texture.

Portions: 4 x Snacks

400g tin chickpeas
1 tsp paprika
1 tsp turmeric
1 tsp ground cumin
3 tbsp olive oil

Make sure to pat your chickpeas very dry to achieve that ultimate crunch!

1 Preheat the oven to 200°C.

2 Drain, rinse and pat the chickpeas dry.

3 Place them on a roasting tray.

4 In a bowl, combine all the spices and mix.

5 Drizzle the chickpeas with the oil and sprinkle on the spices. Toss to ensure that they are evenly coated.

6 Roast for 35-40 minutes until crispy and golden.

7 Eat immediately, or store for up to 3 days in airtight portion pots.

PERFECT FOR TUMMIES | 9 MONTHS+

Biscotti with Babyccino

Healthy Snacks & Treats

This recipe is ideal for teething babies. They are a salt-free alternative to shop bought biscuits, and so can be served as a finger food for your little one. Be sure to serve them with warm frothy milk, otherwise known as 'Babyccino', for a delicious child-friendly treat.

Portions: 18 x Biscuits

125g plain flour
100g wholemeal flour
2 tsp baking powder
½ tsp ground cinnamon
2 eggs, whisked
1 egg yolk
1 tbsp full fat milk

Store any extras in an airtight container for up to one week.

1 Preheat the oven to 180°C and line a baking tray with parchment paper.

2 In a large bowl, mix together all of the dry ingredients. Slowly add the whisked eggs and mix together until a dough starts to form.

3 Split the dough into two, and shape into logs on your baking tray.

4 Mix the egg yolk and the milk together. Using a pastry brush, glaze the logs.

5 Bake in the oven for 20-25 minutes, until golden brown. Remove from the oven and allow to cool for 5-6 minutes before slicing into biscotti shapes.

6 Lower your oven to 160°C then return the biscotti to the baking tray. Bake for a further 15-20 minutes, until dried and golden brown. Remove from the oven and place on a wire rack to cool.

PERFECT FOR TUMMIES | 6 MONTHS+

Frozen Yoghurt Covered Blueberries

This healthy little snack is suitable for weaning babies who are more advanced with finger foods. It's a delicious frozen snack that the children will definitely love!

Portions: 2 x Snacks

125g blueberries
250g natural full fat yoghurt

Vary it each time with other berries like strawberries & raspberries.

1 Wash your blueberries. Line a baking tray with parchment paper and set aside.

2 Insert a kebab stick into one of the blueberries and swirl in the yoghurt until covered.

3 Place on the tray and repeat until all the blueberries are covered.

4 Place the blueberries in the freezer and freeze for one hour.

5 Once they are solid, remove them from the tray and place the blueberries into your portion pots.

6 Allow to come to room temperature before offering to your baby. Store in the fridge for up to one week.

FREEZER FRIENDLY

PERFECT FOR TUMMIES | 9 MONTHS+

Child Friendly Energy Balls

These healthy energy balls are the perfect bite sized snack for your little ones. They are ideal for an after school snack, in between activities or in their lunch boxes to keep them going through busy days. This recipe is only suitable for a babies over 12 months because of the addition of honey.

Portions: 12 x Balls

140g porridge oats
250g cashew butter
4 tbsp honey
75g desiccated coconut
80g ground flaxseed
75g raisins
1 tsp vanilla extract

1 Put all the ingredients into your food processor and blend until combined.

2 Remove from the food processor and shape into bite sized balls.

3 Store in airtight portion pots for up to one week or freeze for future use.

Insert some ice lolly sticks or sturdy straws to make them into pops!

 FREEZER FRIENDLY

PERFECT FOR TUMMIES | 12 MONTHS+

Healthy Kids' Smoothies

Healthy Snacks & Treats

Getting children excited about cooking is not always easy, so making their experience as engaging and fun as possible is key. Creating something together, like a fruit smoothie, is a great way to reward creativity and get your children thinking about healthy alternatives to unhealthy options.

Here are 3 delicious smoothie recipes that I often prepare with my children. Simply blend all the ingredients together until smooth. Freeze the leftovers in ice lolly moulds, as they are great to have on hand when the sun comes out.

For a younger baby, spoon-feed the smoothie. For an older baby, try using a straw.

Yellow Smoothie

This smoothie is full of bright citrus flavours. Your child will love the sweetness of the mango.

230ml orange juice
3 tbsp natural full fat yoghurt
½ mango

Chocolate Smoothie

If your children love chocolate, this smoothie is perfect.

2 frozen bananas
120ml full fat milk
2 tbsp cocoa powder
2 tbsp honey (omit for baby)

Jessica's Smoothie

Jessica loves chosing her own ingredients. This ensures that she will enjoy her smoothie.

1 apple, peeled and chopped
Handful of frozen mixed berries
Handful of pineapple chunks
Handful of fresh strawberries
Small glass of orange juice

 FREEZER FRIENDLY

PERFECT FOR TUMMIES | 6 MONTHS+

Pink Lemonade

—— ••• ——

This pink lemonade is such a treat. Deliciously refreshing, it's the perfect summer drink for hot days. You can even freeze this in moulds to make homemade ice lollies.

Portions: 4 x Glasses

3 stalks rhubarb
4 tbsp caster sugar
6-8 blackcurrants
4 lemons
200ml sparkling water

1 Cut the rhubarb into small pieces. Rinse off and place in a saucepan, along with the sugar and enough water to cover the bottom of the pan.

2 On a low heat with the lid on, stew for 5-10 minutes, until all of the rhubarb breaks down and the sugar dissolves.

3 Add in the blackcurrants and cook for a further 5 minutes. Remove from the heat and allow to cool before passing through a sieve.

4 Juice the lemons in a separate bowl.

5 Combine the rhubarb juice with the lemon juice then add sparkling water, taking care not to dilute it too much!

❄ FREEZER FRIENDLY

PERFECT FOR TUMMIES | 12 MONTHS+

Mixed Berry Nice Cream

Healthy Snacks & Treats

This mixed berry nice cream is a great alternative to shop bought ice cream and contains only 3 ingredients. If you are making this for your weaning baby, substitute the maple syrup for naturally sweet apple purée or fresh apple juice.

Portions: 4 x Child

600g frozen mixed berries
400g natural full fat yoghurt
4 tbsp maple syrup

1 Add all of the ingredients to your blender and blend until smooth.

2 Taste to see if the mixture is sweet enough for your liking, adding more maple syrup if needed or another spoonful of yoghurt if too sweet.

3 If the mixture is frozen to your liking, serve immediately. If not, place in your freezer for 25-30 minutes before serving.

> You can make many versions of nice cream. Try using frozen bananas or peanut butter.

 FREEZER FRIENDLY

PERFECT FOR TUMMIES | 9 MONTHS+

Green Smoothie & Ice Lollies

Healthy Snacks & Treats

Green smoothies are a delicious way of getting greens into your child's diet. They also make great ice lollies for children and teething babies. Get the children involved in making these. They will feel that extra bit of satisfaction while enjoying them.

Portions: 8 x Ice Lollies

1 banana
1 pineapple
1 mango
2 large handfuls of spinach
1 small glass of cold water

1 Place all the ingredients into a smoothie maker or blender and blend until everything is combined.

2 Pour a glass for yourself to enjoy. Place the rest into ice lolly moulds and pop into the freezer.

This is a quick way to boost your child's immune system when they're feeling under the weather.

 FREEZER FRIENDLY

PERFECT FOR TUMMIES | 6 MONTHS+

Very Berry Yoghurt Pops

---•••---

Healthy Snacks & Treats

These homemade popsicles will become your new favourite summer treat! Naturally sweet and creamy, they are perfect for children and teething babies.

Portions: 8 x Ice Pops

125g blackberries
125g raspberries
5 tbsp orange juice
500ml Greek yoghurt

1 In a small bowl, use a fork to mash the blackberries and raspberries.

2 Stir in the orange juice.

3 Place a small amount of the berry mix in the bottom of each mould, before spooning some Greek yoghurt on top. Layer the berries and yoghurt into each mould until all the mixture has been used up.

4 Place in the freezer to set and enjoy later once ready.

5 If you are serving this to a small baby, it's best to blend the berries before adding them to the mixture.

❄ FREEZER FRIENDLY

PERFECT FOR TUMMIES | 6 MONTHS+

Courgette & Peanut Butter Muffins

This sugar free treat is perfect for the whole family, including your weaning baby. It's a great way to include some vegetables and your children will love the icing on top. If anyone has a nut allergy, swap the peanut butter for pumpkin seed butter.

Portions: 6 x Muffins

Muffins
300g raisins
1 courgette
2 heaped tbsp peanut butter
1 egg
4 tbsp oat flour
½ tsp baking powder

Icing
3 tbsp Greek yoghurt
2 tbsp peanut butter

1 Preheat the oven to 180°C. Line a muffin tin with six paper cases and set aside.

2 Add the raisins to a bowl. Cover with boiling water, soak for 5 minutes and then blend. Set aside.

3 In a large bowl, grate the courgette then mix in the peanut butter, egg and ⅔ of the puréed raisins.

4 Next, gently fold in the oat flour and baking powder. Leave to set for 5 minutes.

5 Bake for 20-25 minutes, until golden and cooked through.

6 Remove the muffins from the tin and allow to cool on a wire rack before icing or storing.

7 For the icing: Whip together the yoghurt, remaining raisin purée and peanut butter in a small bowl until smooth. To thicken, mix in a spoon of oat flour and set aside.

8 Once cooled slightly, top the muffins with icing and serve.

 FREEZER FRIENDLY

PERFECT FOR TUMMIES | 6 MONTHS+

First Birthday Smash Cake

Healthy Snacks & Treats

Your baby's first birthday is an exciting time and it's often tempting to get them a sugary cake. Having avoided foods high in sugar while weaning your baby, it's important to stick to a healthy food regime. The last thing you want is your little one having an energy spike followed by a crash on their big day. Instead, celebrate your baby's first birthday with this healthy, sugar free smash cake recipe. Don't be afraid to let them get stuck in!

Portions: 12 x Slices

Cake
4-5 ripe bananas, peeled
2 small apples, stewed and puréed
3 tsp vanilla extract
300g wholemeal flour
1 tsp baking powder
1 tsp cinnamon
¼ tsp nutmeg

Icing
230g cream cheese
2 tsp vanilla extract
50g raisins

1. Preheat the oven to 180°C. Line a medium sized square or number one cake tin and set aside. Cover the raisins in 130ml of warm water for 30 minutes.

2. In a mixing bowl mash the bananas. Add the vanilla extract, and apple purée and mix well. In a separate bowl, mix the flour, baking powder, cinnamon and nutmeg.

3. Fold the wet ingredients into the dry ingredients.

4. Spread the batter evenly into the tin then bake for 30 minutes, until golden and cooked through. Once cooked, remove from the oven and leave to cool on a wire rack.

5. For the icing: Remove the raisins from the juice and discard. Keep the syrup that forms. In a bowl, whisk the cream cheese, raisin juice and vanilla extract, until smooth and creamy.

6. Decorate as desired with your favourite toppings. I love adding fruits such as blueberries, strawberries and raspberries.

 FREEZER FRIENDLY

PERFECT FOR TUMMIES | 6 MONTHS+

It doesn't end here

・・・

I hope you will have a wonderful weaning journey with your little one. My support doesn't end here. Head over to my site at **MummyCooks.com** for the latest recipes and advice for the entire family.

@mummycooks

I would love to see how you put my recipes and products to use! Snap and send me your pictures and reviews using **#mummycooks** on social media.

Sign up now at www.MummyCooks.com and
get 10% off your next order!

✓ Recipes perfect for Baby & Family
✓ Advice & Tips ✓ Offers ✓ Competitions

Index

About Siobhan Berry

Siobhan Berry founded Mummy Cooks in 2012 as the first baby weaning cookery school in Ireland. It was her mission to empower and educate mums about weaning with healthy, homemade food so their little ones would grow into happy, healthy and adventurous eaters. It has since grown into an international online business offering advice, recipes and award-winning feeding and weaning products.

Through her years in the feeding and weaning industry, she has been named the resident feeding and weaning expert with MummyPages.ie, Ireland's largest parenting website, and as a brand ambassador for SuperValu on the 'Let's Get Ireland Cooking' campaign. She has become synonymous with weaning and feeding children throughout the country.

Siobhan currently lives in Dublin with her husband, Dave, and her two daughters, Ashleigh and Jessica.

Notes